THE ROME-BERLIN-TOKIO AXIS.
THIS MAP SHOWS THE STRATEGICAL COMMAND EXERCISED BY THE AXIS VIS-A-VIS THE BRITISH EMPIRE.

Can Chamberlain Save Britain?

"AYE, AYE, SIR!"

SIR ANTHONY EDEN [*sic*] SMILINGLY AGREES WITH
M. LITVINOFF AT THE NINE POWER CONFERENCE IN
BRUSSELS

*This photograph appeared with the above caption in the "New York
Sun" on Saturday, November 20, 1937. It is an interesting
indication of the view taken of Mr. Eden's motives in foreign policy
by American observers*

CAN CHAMBERLAIN
SAVE BRITAIN?

The Lesson of Munich

By

COLLIN BROOKS

1938

EYRE & SPOTTISWOODE

First printed . . 1938

PRINTED IN GREAT BRITAIN FOR
EYRE AND SPOTTISWOODE (PUBLISHERS) LIMITED

CONTENTS

FOREWORD

THE Four Power Conference of Munich in September 1938 gave to the world either an uneasy postponement of conflict or the promise of a lasting peace.

There have been many interpretations placed upon it. Many will agree with the Prime Minister that the most vital aspect of his three visits to Germany was the demonstration that the German people want peace, despite the militarism of the régime under which they live. Others will agree that Munich showed that the heads of "Democratic" States can talk directly and with amicable results with the heads of Totalitarian States. All must be aware that it was a demonstration of the real power of Germany, since for the third time the Prime Minister of Great Britain flew hurriedly to the presence of the ruler of Germany in an effort to persuade him not to make war, bringing with him the Premier of France and— at Britain's solicitation—the Duce of Italy. Palatable or unpalatable, the fact is that ill-prepared and loosely organised democratic States waited upon well-prepared and tightly-organised Totalitarian States.

Before the advent to power of Herr Hitler my published writings on national affairs were critical of the power of Parliament, that is of the Parliamentary

system as we have come to work it, to protect
Britain from disaster, whether military or economic.
After the rise of Herr Hitler, that view was uttered
more and more stridently by me. As early as 1935
I incurred great odium by publishing in a popular
newspaper a frank plea for National Service. As
early as 1934—I am a little amazed to find—in the
very mild forum of *The Bookman*, least controversial
of papers, I was urging that democracy must spell
national doom in the face of Hitlerism. Throughout
1936, both in the daily Press and the strongly contrasted pages of *The English Review*, I declared in the
face of much ridicule that Britain economically
was again infested with the virus of 1929. This book
repeats and develops all that I wrote in those earlier
years. It is a book written in the sincere conviction
that the prime need of the world is peace, and that
of all nations Great Britain can least afford war.
It is written in the belief that the economic no less
than the military circumstances of Great Britain
have radically changed during the past two generations, and that the change of circumstances demands
a change of policy if Britain is to survive as the heart
of a great Empire.

There is much in the pages that follow which can
be glibly labelled "defeatism" or stamped as lack of
patriotism. In stating and asking others to face
unpleasant truths I am conscious of neither defeatism
nor lack of patriotism. On the contrary, I believe
that those Parliamentarians and publicists in the
Press who have misled the public as to the relative

military strengths of the nations and the relative economic soundness of Britain and her trade rivals will, in the light of coming events, incur the gravest responsibility. They will have helped to leave the nation unprepared for facts very different from the more palatable fancies woven from complacent imaginations.

In the Spring of 1938 I published a small book called "Can 1931 Come Again?" in which I drew attention to the consistent and rapid decay of our export industries, to the coming decline in our invisible exports, to the unsound growth of national and municipal debt and to the appalling neglect of our native agriculture. The book was widely reviewed and discussed, but commentators, with a few exceptions, refused to admit that Britain was driving to a crisis. Their refusal was based upon a belief that a currency unanchored from gold could prevent any such repetition of the debacle of 1931. Trade figures, traffic figures, company results, bank clearings have, since the publication of that book, steadily and monotonously confirmed its forecasts. In July 1938 a meeting of Members of Parliament under the auspices of the 1922 Committee allowed to be put on public record its opinion that a financial crisis was virtually inevitable between 1939 and 1940. In the same month the heads of two great shipping companies publicly announced that they could not place orders for British ships as British prices were uneconomic. The general consciousness of the country, it is obvious, is now receptively aware of those grim facts

which were scouted when "Can 1931 Come Again?"
was published.

What that small volume did for the economic phase
only of our national life, this book attempts to do for
a broader political aspect.   For any abuse which it
may arouse, I care nothing.   For any reasoned and
constructive criticism which it draws, proving some
of my more gloomy beliefs to be fallacious, I offer in
advance a sincere welcome.

One section of the early chapters in particular I
would wish to emphasise.   For many years past, in
newspaper articles, in books, in reviews of other
men's books, in speeches and addresses, I have denounced Parliamentary Government, as we know it,
as a decadent and inefficient institution.   Such an
attitude towards Parliament, as that sturdy old
democrat Mr. George Bernard Shaw has recently
discovered, immediately classifies a man as a friend
to tyranny and a lover of dictatorship.   I am no
friend to tyranny and no lover of tyrants—but,
unfortunately, I am compelled to realise that the swift
and secret progress towards a chosen aim which is
possible to dictators and is not possible to Parliaments, the devotion and sacrifice of sectional interests
to national advancement which is possible to dictator
countries and is apparently not possible to Parliamentary democracies, places Parliamentary countries
at a grave and probably a fatal disadvantage,
whether for military or economic triumph.   Unless
and until that disadvantage is remedied Great Britain
must remain in the jeopardy in which we now see her.

That is the conviction which is the essence of this book.

There is one other accusation to which this book is almost certain to give rise. It is that its writer is an enemy of the British worker, desiring to limit freedom and reduce material comforts. It is because I care above all else for the survival of the British worker and desire to preserve him from the greatest and most cruel of catastrophes—the assault and destruction of modern war and the starvation and misery of economic collapse—that I have tried to assemble the facts of our recent and present history and to draw from them what seem to me to be the inevitable conclusions.

I do not believe that Britain is finished—but I do believe that without a drastic reform of her methods of Government and her mode of living her existence as a great Power must be further imperilled, and may be ended. To suggest that whatever curtailment of individual liberty and whatever sacrifice of immediate material comfort such a reform demands is too great a price to pay for security and survival seems to me a betrayal of those masses of people not in a position to know or interpret the facts, and a negation of sense.

To disguise the facts or wilfully to misinterpret them because electors, shareholders or newspaper subscribers may not relish unpalatable truths seems to me, as I wrote in my previous book, to be rank cowardice. It is cowardice of that kind which invites disaster because it lulls into a false sense of security those who should be active in their own defence.

It was such cowardice that misled the British people about their relative weakness in the air when Germany had re-armed. It was such cowardice that permitted the ordeal of 1931 to affect many hundreds of thousands of British homesteads without warning or time to prepare for its hardships.

External circumstances and not national desires to-day govern Britain's course. She may choose between a generation of discipline and frugality and a generation of prodigality and peril. The first may lead to a new prosperity and, combined with a realistic foreign policy, to a new security. The second will assuredly lead to economic bankruptcy and possibly to political destruction.

These are grave words—but, at the moment, no more than words.

By the *facts* that follow they must be justified or refuted. In the presentation of those facts I have tried to be honest; in my interpretation of them I am certainly sincere. Of the reader who considers them, whether in agreement or disagreement with my conclusions, I solicit the same honesty and sincerity of purpose—the good of Britain and the welfare and survival of her people.

C. B.

October 1938.

CHAPTER I

BRITAIN AT HAZARD

Time and the ocean and some fostering star
In high cabal have made us what we are . . .
WILLIAM WATSON.

WHATEVER view is taken of the events of September 1938, when the vigour and courage of Neville Chamberlain snatched Europe from the very brink of destruction by war, one fact is beyond dispute. Germany, as Herr Hitler told the British Prime Minister, was ready to face a world war, and Britain was not.

Had the Godesberg ultimatum not been softened at Munich, Britain would have fought—but under appalling handicaps. Imminent war revealed to the most complacent self-comforters how great were the gaps in our defences.

Mr. Chamberlain has been arraigned as one of those responsible for the perilous plight in which Great Britain found herself. It is a charge from which he cannot wholly escape, for it was he who stood at the right hand of Mr. Stanley Baldwin and Mr. Ramsay MacDonald during the years when the British people were misled as to the strength of German armaments and were themselves left without adequate preparation for a clash which the British Government's own foreign policy had made almost inevitable.

By the Summer of 1938 it was obvious that after

emerging as a victorious Power from the War of 1914–1918 Britain in twenty years had sunk so low in international prestige that she could with impunity be insulted, ignored and derided. Italy, Germany, Japan, Fascist Spain had all in turn shown unmistakably, as this book will later demonstrate, that neither Britain's wrath nor her honest indignation caused any perturbation among those who knew that their arms and determination outweighed those of the British.

Mr. Chamberlain's insistence over Czechoslovakia on a negotiated settlement, and his ability to convince Herr Hitler, even at the eleventh hour, that Britain was prepared to accept war rather than see the forms of negotiation set aside, has temporarily improved Britain's prestige with Germany. But that prestige cannot be maintained now that our total unpreparedness for war has been so mercilessly exposed.

Mr. Chamberlain, fortunately, at Godesberg and Munich had not to press his opposition to Germany far.

Czechoslovakia was not a worthy occasion for war. Under President Benes the Czechs, far from forming a noble little democracy as British sentimentalists supposed, represented a tyrannous government, oppressive to its minorities, and dominated in international politics by Russia. Czechoslovakia was created in chicanery and existed in tyranny. Its dismemberment was not a wrong, but the righting of a wrong. But the lesson of that dismemberment was that Europe yielded to a threat of force what had been refused to appeals to justice, and she yielded because Soviet Russia, half-Communist France and unarmed-Britain were unable to contemplate a conflict with the Totalitarian States. It was not the fear of bombs over Prague, but of bombs over London and Paris that caused the great wave of anti-war feeling in the British and French capitals, neither of which was equipped to defend its peoples.

The lesson of the recent crisis drives deeper than any realisation that Britain's rearmament has been tardy and inefficient. It raises the question whether Britain in the modern world can survive without a complete change in her mode of life.

Mr. Chamberlain in roughly a year of office has done much to reverse and repair the errors of policy which had caused the decay of British power and influence—but there still remains for the British people the real choice of ways.

Are they to cling tenaciously from mere sentiment to outworn forms and modes of Government no longer capable of protecting the State from military or economic disaster, or are they to abandon such obsolete forms for a system of Government which will preserve the State and ensure the continuance of the Empire?

It is the habit of many hearty but thoughtless patriots to preach that any weakness detected in the situation of Britain is more apparent than real, that in the jaundiced eye of the critic, and not in the fabric of the Constitution he examines, is the flaw. The Empire, they cry, is virile. It cannot perish.

Such Imperial *Couéism* cannot save the British Commonwealth if it is left open to its enemies, whether those enemies be the airmen of political adversaries or the ideologies of its own sections.

Every man feels that all men are mortal but himself. Great Empires entering their epochs of destruction are no less sure of survival, though Empires as great have passed, slowly or swiftly, from domination. Historians and philosophers have combined to explore the causes which bring Empires to ruin, and they have agreed that the popular idea that races lose power from the onset of age is not sound.

It is not true that there are young and virile nations and old and decrepit ones. Empires have perished with their peoples still in vigour. Racial decadence *may* cause destruction, but there are other causes.

"We must not consider a diminution of national power, whether relative or absolute, as constituting by itself a proof of national decadence," said a famous statesman-philosopher.* "Holland is not decadent because her place in the hierarchy of European Powers is less exalted than it was two hundred years ago. Spain was not necessarily decadent at the end of the seventeenth century because she had exhausted herself in a contest far beyond her resources either in money or men. It would, I think, be rash even to say that Venice was decadent at the end of the eighteenth century, though the growth of other Powers, and the diversion of the great trade routes, had shorn her of wealth and

*Lord Balfour: "Sidgwick Memorial Lecture," Cambridge, 1908.

international influence. These are misfortunes which
in the sphere of sociology correspond to accident or
disease in the sphere of biology."

To say, and feel, that the future of Britain is dark
and doubtful is not to say that the British are
necessarily decadent. It is rather to say that,
whether virile or decadent, the British have shown
in the last score of years that they are no more
immune from "accident" than were Holland, Spain
or Venice, and to express the fear that by lethargy or
blunder they are now inviting calamities which can
and should be avoided.

Britain is unique among nations. Only Japan
remotely resembles her. The means of the British
rise to dominance and the needs which Britain has
for vast necessary imports to ensure the survival of
her too dense population are shared in the history
and circumstance of no other race.

Even the qualities of the Briton are peculiar. No
other race can show that strange mixture of assurance
of its own selfless sincerity combined with the
conviction abroad of its selfish hypocrisy. With the
Bible in one hand and the sword in the other or by a
combination of missionary zeal and shrewd dealing
the Briton has taken to himself a quarter of the
habitable globe and claims dominion over all its
waters, and this he has done in the name of humanity,
unaware, or resentful, that humanity regards his
search for invisible grace as being strangely like a
search for invisible exports.

To-day, with his possession threatened and his

2

claim to domination challenged, the Briton turns on the qualities which won him his Empire and his high standards of material and cultural living, and denounces them in others as signs of barbarism.

In considering the choice that lies before Britain let us at the outset clear our minds of one piece of cant. Having made an Empire, and having permitted an industrial revolution to create a population of over forty-seven millions of people for islands ill adapted naturally to support half that number, we cannot now decide that "property is theft" and that Imperialism is criminal.

We are the legatees of our own responsibilities. Our millions must be fed and defended, no matter how much any of them may yearn for some new and gentler ideal of life. We cannot say, "this is not the Britain of our dream—to Hell with it." We can find no answer when other nations, finding us in a mood of new moral self-righteousness, ready to rebuke in others the aspirations we once applauded in ourselves, cry, scornfully, "Dost thou think, because thou art virtuous, there shall be no more cakes and ale!"

"Time, and the ocean and some fostering star" are not alone responsible for the shape our racial destiny has taken. Necessary adventurers like Raleigh and Drake, Clive, Hastings and Rhodes, Wolfe and Strathcona, Edward Gibbon Wakefield and John Nicholson, have aided in making us what we are. We need for our very existence the kind of Britain that they made for us.

If we now deprecate the qualities of these ancestors and hold their legacy in contempt, we shall assuredly find that men of their mould, speaking other tongues, will rend the heritance from us.* If that happens, we perish, some of our millions dying and others passing into helotry.

The choice, in short, is not between the Britain that we know and some more pleasant Britain fashioned from a pipe-dream of Utopia. It is between the Britain that we know, with all its incessant economic needs, and a vassal Britain warped and disciplined by minds alien to our traditions.

I have said that Britain is unique among nations. She is unique in this, that her topographical location, her geographical circumstance, gave to her in the days before steam a position of especial command. Situated just North of Europe when the tide of European civilisation had flowed northwards from the original cradle of mankind, the Mediterranean basin, and due East of the American continent, when the new world, as men called it, was beginning to demand the men and services of the old world, the British Isles were placed to receive, indeed, the best of both worlds.

A group of islands set in Northern seas, but granted, from the fortuitous course of the Gulf Stream, a climate that combined the warmth that makes men genial and the cold that makes them energetic, had perforce to breed a race of industrious agriculturalists, of skilled and daring seamen and of adventurous wayfarers. Few races have owed more to their environment than the British.

*If any doubt this, let them realise that Drake and Balbo are alike celebrated in history as great circumnavigators of the globe.

To the making of the British character heredity no
less than environment contributed.   The stocks that
were crossed to produce the racial types which set
sail to wrest an Empire for Britain from other nations
and from the unexplored places of the world were
vigorous stocks.   Had they not been so, they would
never have come to the northern isles.

Four great cultures had waxed and waned in the
British Isles before the coming of the Romans, who
ruled here for four hundred years with their gift of a
highly ordered and cultivated society.   The Roman
legions left the Wall, and the Picts came flooding
from the North.   To stem this tide, what still
remained of Roman Britain sought or welcomed the
help of strong fighting men from the regions round
Denmark.   By the eighth century the Danes themselves were pouring into Britain.   From the great
raid of 787, when the viking freebooters devastated
Northumbria, to the day when Swegen handed the
sceptre of Britain to his son Canute in the eleventh
century, the tide of battle swirled between Saxons
and Danes, until Edward the Confessor and Harold,
last of the Saxon kings, gave place to the arrogant
Norman whom we have come to call William the
Conqueror and they knew as the Bastard of Falaise.

For over a thousand years the British Isles
received, and absorbed or slew, these fighting
breeds—Celt, Roman, Saxon, Dane, Norseman,
Norman—each contributing a strain, while visiting
traders from the far ends of the then known
earth impregnated the tradition, and doubtless the

physique of the race, with minor but potent influences.

The work of the Norman kings—the last of the raiders, the raiders who came to stay—in welding the people of the islands into a nation is the commonplace of every child's history book, but in admiring the work of the welders none should forget or underrate the materials welded.

A people so fashioned, in a land so set, were well equipped to fulfil the national destiny of Britain before the days of steam; they were even more favoured when steam, like a djinn from a bottle, transformed the political and trading aspects of the world.

Until the industrial revolution Britain's staple manufacture was cloth. Thereafter she began to concentrate on all kinds of industry, but particularly textiles, coal mining and the many departments of the iron and steel trade. Because she had vast resources of coal and iron, *and no coal or iron field was far from a port*, she was first in the field as a modern manufacturing nation. Until relatively recent years she was to retain her unchallenged position as the workshop of the world.

Added to the luck of her geographical position and the possession of coal and iron was the extra luck of the social system which had developed before the invention of the steam engine.

"It was essential that there should be Capital which was necessary to finance the new methods of production—and, of course, men willing to use their capital in this way—in order to make them a business proposition. Trade and commerce were thus indispensable preliminaries to industrialism, and these had been well developed in England by the eighteenth century. On the one hand, there was a certain number of men who had made great fortunes in foreign trade; and, on the other hand, there was a very considerable number of people who, by means of thrift, had accumulated small fortunes in industry and trade, though the scale of their operations had not been extensive. Never was the inequality of the distribution of wealth so fortunate. As soon as the new methods were conclusively proved to be economically sound—though this was not immediately done—the necessary money was forthcoming. But it may be noticed that it was the man with only a moderate amount of capital who came forward rather than the nabob, who preferred to invest his money in land, which gave political power and dignity. As a rule, the industrialist was a nonconformist who had amassed money by hard work and abstinence, whilst the nabob-cum-landowner was a member of the Church of England and a luxury lover. The theological views of the new industrialist were of especial importance. He believed that the parable of the talents was the basis of the Christian life, and that, if he had the opportunity, it was his first religious duty to make a material success of life by exploiting those to whom God had given inferior gifts."

It is thus that Mr. Frederic Milner emphasises (in his "Economic Evolution in England") an aspect of the economic development of Britain which cannot be over-emphasised, although it is often overlooked.

The first British Empire, which was made between the days of the Tudors and the end of the eighteenth century, had been created by necessary adventurers, ranked by the outer world as pirates and filibusters, whose homeland was in a fortunate position as the base of their raids and wars. Of this period Francis Drake and Robert Clive can be taken as the representative men.

The second British Empire, which overlapped the first by a few years, was made possible by the same lucky positioning of the British Isles, by the presence there of essential raw materials for the exploitation of the new discoveries in the application of steam, by the absence of strong competitors, and by a peculiar turn of national character. That character had been moulded from the mixed stocks of adventurous men who had successively invaded and ruled Britain by the interplay of certain religious and political forces.

This, then, is to be marked—that if by the opening up of new lands in distant parts of the world Britain's geographical relation to her markets changes and is no longer first in advantage, if new sources of power and new forms of raw material supplant the iron and coal of Britain's great age, and if the national character loses the hard strains, the mixture of thrift and courage that once distinguished it, Britain is doomed.

Britain's geographical relation to her markets *has* changed. For more than a century now the "New

World" has provided markets and suppliers to outweigh the old.

New sources of power, water, oil, and electricity, *have* supplanted the coal and iron of Britain's great age.

New raw materials *are* beginning to supplant the iron and steel of that flourishing time. Already cellulose made from timber and milk, new aluminium alloys and other contrivances of science are usurping the places held by the older simple metals and textiles.

Has the national character changed also? Young men who vote and boast that under no pressure of circumstances will they fight for King and Country, old men who relinquish the economic and political control of vast dependencies like India, Egypt and the Middle-East while yet bearing the responsibility for their defence, emotional mobs that scream with anger against the thrust and drive of more virile nations and yet refuse to arm against them—are these, indeed, signs of a decay of national character that will add the last ingredient to the chalice of our racial destruction?

It is this question in particular that this book sets itself to examine. From this question arises the second, that if the national character is still capable of preserving what it once created, is the system by which the nation is governed adequate for the task?

Those who ask this kind of question are, I know, in danger of being accused of lack of patriotism. They are open to the charge of being bewitched by

Berchtesgaden. They are immediately derided as the
foes of democracy and liberty. My own conscience
is clear. I know that the parrot cry of "Liberty!" is
deadly if it means the liberty to refuse to make an
effort to safeguard the means of all liberty, which is
national security.

As for patriotism—what but a very genuine
patriotism would cause a man to risk, as in this and
other works *I* risk, the odium and derision of complacent and unawakened minds by the bawling of
unpalatable truths about the jeopardy in which the
country reels?

In asking "Whither Britain?" I see what Cobbett
saw, and

> what he saw was the perishing of the whole English power
> of self-support, the growth of cities that drain and dry up the
> countryside, the growth of dense dependent populations
> incapable of finding their own food, the toppling triumph of
> machines over men, the sprawling omnipotence of financiers
> over patriots, the herding of humanity in nomadic masses
> whose very homes are homeless, the terrible necessity of
> peace and the terrible probability of war, all the loading up
> of our little island like a sinking ship; the wealth that may
> mean famine and the culture that may mean despair; the
> bread of Midas and the sword of Damocles.*

But what Cobbett saw, with his foresight, when our
peril began, I see as much more imminent, as our
peril reaches its climax.

If Great Britain is forced or lured into war without
adequate arms and with her people undrilled to take
the shock of attack, our end is certain. It is the

*"William Cobbett," G. K. Chesterton.

vassalage of which I have spoken. But if "the terrible probability of war" remains only a probability, our fate is in our own hands. A refusal to change our methods of Government and our mode of life may mean our destruction; a determination to assess the forces at work in a world of political and economic transition, and to adapt our forms of Government and our ways of living to their dread necessity, may mean a triumphant survival in the face of all inimical circumstances.

Never in all our fretted history were our fortunes so much at hazard. If Britain *must* perish, it is the hope of this book that no cenotaph shall remind our conquerors that fetish worship and false pride, love of comfort and fear of sacrifice betrayed us.

Chapter II

TOWARDS BANKRUPTCY

The Association of British Chambers of Commerce, meeting in
Glasgow yesterday, October 6th 1938, adopted a resolution viewing
with considerable anxiety the existing world conditions and their
effect upon our export trade. " We in this country must starve
if we do not export," said Mr. Harry Alcock of Manchester.

NEWS CHRONICLE, October 7th, 1938.

Over-spending, lack of home productivity, lack of competitive
power in foreign markets, high costs, rising and crippling taxation,
declining revenue from overseas investments and shipping services—
all these face us as they faced us in 1931.   They are now, as then, the
sure signs of impending crisis.   And to-day we have serious foreign
complications that were absent in 1931.

" CAN 1931 COME AGAIN?"

ALTHOUGH in dramatic periods of history
foreign policy and the danger of war over-
shadows other less exciting aspects of the
national life, foreign policy must itself be governed
by the economic capacity of the nation to impose its
will on others or to prevent others imposing their
will on it.

Britain's strength for many generations was her
industrial wealth. The creation of that wealth
transformed the British Isles from rural communities
to congested centres of industrial workers and their
commercial assistants.

In the early days of Britain's rise to world power
the people of the islands were able to feed themselves
and clothe themselves with relative ease, even though
the nation might be locked in a death struggle, as it
was with Spain and as it was in the days of Napoleon

15

with France. But with the coming of steam power, and those other sources of power which have followed steam, this self-reliance passed.

To-day the crux of all policy is that some 47,000,000 of people must be supported in all circumstances and must command sufficient overseas trade to make that support possible in addition to any cost of defence. A vigorous foreign policy must always carry in its wake the possibility of war. War to-day implies the cutting off of those millions from their normal sources of supplies. But what is just as sinister is that a steady decay of trade may render the nation unable to purchase those supplies in the necessary quantity, war or no war.

By all the reliable indices to trade, we are now suffering such a decay. In the course of one long lifetime the whole problem of the British Government has completely changed. Where there was once a nation of great and increasing economic power and wealth, able by a great navy to blockade the ports of an enemy, there is now a nation of decreasing wealth whose own ports can be blockaded.

The modern statesman must take this position as he finds it. He cannot change it. It is his terrible inheritance. With such a background to his foreign policy he dare not make wanton enemies whose ill will must adversely affect the nation's trade.

The change to an industrial State dependent upon foreign supplies for the sustenance of a crowded population was not quick. Discussing British

industry as late as 1851, Professor Clapham* says
of it:

> Britain had turned her face towards the new industry—
> the wheels of iron and the shriek of the escaping steam. In
> them lay for the future not only her power and wealth, but
> her very existence. She must take the risks of the "industry
> state," which lives by the export of its manufactures,
> because she could do no other. Many Englishmen bore those
> risks proudly, like the industrial free traders of the North.
> Most bore them ignorantly, seeing to-day's cheaper loaf or
> to-morrow's good balance sheet. Educated men of the older
> country stocks were apt to shoulder them with reluctance,
> regretting that not ill-adjusted life of town and country
> which was passing away. Those who had followed Peel with
> open eyes, like Sir James Graham, had done so because
> population was growing "at the rate of 300,000 per annum."
> It had been a question of time, a race between life and food.
> To such men free trade was a need to be faced, not a treasure
> to be won.
>
> The course was set towards the "industry state," but the
> voyage was not half over . . .

Even as late as the eighteen-seventies, when
modern communications had made the world one
market, and Britain was for good or ill a trade and
industry State, home-produced food supplies outweighed imported foodstuffs, but that balance was
rapidly changing, and the increase in population,
mostly dependent on imported raw materials for the
means of livelihood, was increasing at enormous
proportions each year. England and Wales that
in 1801 had had under 9,000,000 to feed and
house, had approximately 18,000,000 in 1851, nearly

*"Economic History of Modern Britain," Vol. 2.

30,000,000 in 1891, over 36,000,000 in 1911 and nearly 39,000,000 in 1921.

By the beginning of the eighteen-nineties a huge balance of payments in Britain's favour was necessary to pay for the absolute necessaries of existence.

To those unacquainted with the processes of trade this may seem a foolish statement. Surely if Britain could either sell goods to the value of those she needed, or could combine the value of goods sold with the value of the shipping, insurance and capital-providing (i.e., investment) services she rendered to other nations, an exact balance would suffice. A favourable balance would not be necessary. In practice that is not sound. Raw materials have to be bought in advance of the sale of the products into which they are manufactured; foodstuffs have to be in store and even consumed before the workers have produced the goods that will eventually result from their labours to pay part of Britain's overseas bill.

The growth of Britain's trade between the opening years of the industrial revolution and the slump of 1929 had increased over 110 times.

The point to mark is this—that whereas Britain in 1750 had sold only £12,750,000 less than she had bought, by 1913 the gap had risen to £123,914,413 and last year to £432,300,000. In 1938 it will probably be £480,000,000. Those gaps have to be made good by what are known as invisible exports, which are the services which Britain can render overseas for which foreigners are able and willing to pay, such as the carrying of goods, the financing of enterprise, the insuring of property, the entertainment of tourists, and the like.

As other nations in turn became industrialised Britain tended to sell less to them of her genuine manufactures and—owing to the system of Free Imports which prevailed in this country—to buy more. For many years Britain's exports kept pace with the industrialisation of her customers because she sold to them the very means of their industrialisation, the textile machines, engines, locomotives and so on which they needed for their own manufactures. She sold, that is, the means which would enable her customers to become her competitors.

Britain's natural command of world trade first passed when her customers were equipped to make those things that Britain had previously supplied, including the means to make them.

It was not, however, until comparatively recently that Britain's command of the world market for her characteristic "invisible exports" began to wane. Even when the great war has caused Britain to dissipate her great pools of credit abroad, London remained the money market of the world and British investment abroad continued to be enormous. Investments abroad yielded an income of £205,000,000 in 1936 and were estimated to yield £220,000,000 in 1937. Shipping was for long an activity in which Britain kept well ahead of all competitors, and from which a great invisible export income was drawn. But whereas in 1914 the British owned tonnage in relation to total world tonnage was (approximately) as 19 is to 45, by 1925 it had dropped to the proportion of 19 to 63 and last year (1937) was only as 17 is to 65*. Shipping is suffering exactly as British manufactures have suffered. We are no longer offering to the world something that the world must have and can get from nobody else.

Shipping and investment income are by far the biggest items in the list of invisible exports. Shipping is not only now declining because of the competition of foreign nations who have put on the water cheaper and swifter vessels, but the income from shipping is declining because we are using ourselves more of the available services, partly from the increase in normal imports to Britain, but largely because of the abnormal import for re-armament.

Investment income threatens to show us a similar shrinkage. Economic distress and political changes have caused and are causing nations to default on their loan payments. They are seizing, either for no payment or for trivial payment, utilities and enterprises for which British capital paid and on which British owners have hitherto drawn interest. The easy examples that come to the mind of varying defaults are those of Brazil through economic distress, Mexico from politico-economic desires to own nationally their own mineral resources, and Germany, who not only refuses to honour the Austrian debt services, but insists upon scaling down the agreed interest on

*The actual figures are :—Total world tonnage, 65,271,000. British-owned tonnage, 17,436,000. These figures refer to gross tonnage of steam and motor ships only.

German loans made by British citizens. In addition to these sources of distress to British income drawers is a shrinkage in the national income from investments abroad caused by British owners of plantations and other enterprises abroad selling to the foreigner and bringing their money home because they fear to keep it in parts of the world where war or revolution may rob them of their possession. It may well be that before these lines see print, large defaults will have been made in the Far East as one of the consequences of the war between Japan and China.

In a nutshell, 1938 sees Britain in this position— that she is continuing to buy more from abroad and sell less, and the invisible exports that should fill the gap in this balance of indebtedness are shrinking with some rapidity.

It is not necessary to labour the fact that countries that in the early days of the machine age were our big customers are no longer big buyers, but one or two examples may make that fact more vivid to the mind. This small table, confined to the years after the recovery from the Great War, is illuminating.

TOTAL EXPORTS OF BRITISH AND IMPORTED MERCHANDISE.

To	1928.	1935.	1936.*
INDIA	£85,087,000	£38,437,000	£34,608,000
CHINA	15,853,000	5,059,000	5,835,000
JAPAN	14,824,000	4,138,000	3,653,000
ARGENTINA	31,776,000	15,607,000	15,540,000

*Latest available year.

TOTAL EXPORTS OF BRITISH AND IMPORTED
MERCHANDISE—*continued.*

To	1928.	1935.	1936*.
†ITALY	16,472,000	8,146,000	941,000
BELGIUM	27,347,000	13,127,000	14,159,000
GERMANY	67,364,000	26,401,000	25,796,000
U.S.A.	68,736,000	30,109,000	36,773,000

Omitting Italy, where special circumstances ruled in the years 1935-6, in every case British sales have fallen heavily, to fractions varying from under ¼ to ½.

The decline of British exports to these countries was obviously not due to the same cause or causes in each case.

Countries like India began to manufacture for themselves in a wide variety of ways. Not only have Indian cotton mills proved strong competitors of Lancashire mills, but India now manufactures all the sugar, matches and practically all the cement she requires‡. In addition, political prejudice against Britain affected what the Americans call "customer good-will."

China and India both found in Japan a cheaper supplier.

Germany first grew poor and unable to buy, and then grew proud and turned to Autarchy to keep her purchases low.

But in all cases Britain was handicapped by two factors—her costs were far higher than those of her

*Latest available year.

†1935 and 1936 show the effects of sanctions, which cost Britain between £8,000,000 and £9,000,000 of trade, helped to ruin some parts of the Empire, like Newfoundland and New Brunswick, and were utterly ineffective.

‡Sir Charles A. Innes at the general meeting of the Bank of India, 1938

competitors and her political policies were not
conducive to friendliness in the customer.

All these aspects of Britain's loss of command
shall be discussed in greater detail later. For the
moment, it is to be noted that:

> Britain's export trade has diminished and is
> diminishing.
> Britain's adverse balance of trade is increasing.
> Britain's income from "invisibles" is now tending
> to shrink.

These things, we have seen, come about largely
because Britain's one-time customers are now able
to supply themselves or to buy cheaper from competitors who were once themselves our customers and
because others are now rendering the services, such
as shipping, which Britons were once paid to perform.

There are the other causes which have only been
mentioned in passing. They are: (1) that oil and
water power, in the form of electricity, have over-
taken steam power for which Britain was once
specially equipped and other nations for the most
part not equipped, and (2) new materials which
Britain does not possess have begun to supplant
those which Britain does possess.

To avoid argument about the effect of the world
slump that began in 1929, let us take some figures
for the year 1928.

In that year Britain imported oil to the value of
over £45,000,000. That means that instead of being
an almost monopolistic supplier of power and lighting

to others, she was herself a debtor for power and
lighting to that amount.

In that year she imported timber to the value of
£42,000,000 whereas she had once been able to
supply from her own lands all the timber she needed.
She bought rubber to the value of £25,000,000. Her
aluminium import was £1,366,719, whereas in 1923 it
was only £274,000 and by 1936 had risen to nearly
£2,000,000.

These figures indicate the reversal of Britain's
trade relation to the outer world compared with the
mid-years of last century, but their significance is
small compared with the fact that every other nation
which now produces or uses aluminium, oil, rubber,
timber and wood-pulps, is by that amount independent of Britain's own types of raw materials,
coal, iron, steel, which were once the basis of her
prosperity.

Britain's loss of a trading command of world
markets is a question of hard, indisputable fact. It
is not a matter of opinion, or of "optimism versus
pessimism," or of patriotism versus non-patriotism.
Political policy may, as we shall shortly discuss, have
accelerated the pace of that loss, but policy did not
cause it. What caused it was the discovery of new
means of living following upon the advance of more
primitive peoples whom Britain was once able to
supply with manufactures.

But whatever the cause, the problem for Britain
is how can the independence of other countries upon
Britain be compensated for by new British methods

or new effort. Britain was able to support her rapidly increasing population by a rapid increase of trade, the one increasing threefold and the other over a hundredfold. But while population still increases, trade has begun to move in a direction that plunges Britain deeper and deeper into the mire of indebtedness.

It cannot continue without catastrophe.

Britain must realise that her old accidental advantages have passed. Many of them, like the possession of desirable raw materials and a favourable topographical location, have passed to her competitors. Others have been cancelled out by circumstances. But Britain continues to "live high." Her workers demand a higher return than the workers of Japan, India and Germany, to name but three of her competitors, with the result that the cost of her goods is such that customers will not buy them. This is not merely a question of higher wages or longer periods of leisure. It is also a question of the many amenities which are added to nominal wages, the free education, the lavishly laid out townships with their subsidised pleasure facilities, the provision of services for the preservation of the public health.

Nobody denies that these things are eminently desirable. Nobody wantonly wishes to deprive the nation of any of them. But desires and wishes are not at the moment our concern, which is the fact that to provide high wages plus amenities there must be a flourishing state of trade, and that trade is no longer flourishing and cannot again flourish as it did when Britain was the workshop of the world.

It will be immediately contended that a high standard of life for the workers *en masse* cannot be criticised while industry pays high levels of profit to the finders of capital. That is perfectly true, but industry no longer pays a high return to capital when the State and the Municipalities have levied their toll. Great incomes to-day yield thirteen shillings and ninepence in every pound to the State in direct taxation, before they begin to pay their share of indirect taxation and the high rates which local taxing bodies demand from them.

To pay for past and present defence and for her various social services Britain has created a national debt of over £7,400,000,000 (of which over £1,000,000,000 is owed overseas) and a local debt of £1,500,000,000. On this total of £8,900,000,000 interest has to be found as a standing overhead charge on British industry, a sum in the neighbourhood of £250,000,000 a year. Our native industry has to find this sum before it begins to raise around £700,000,000 current expenditure and to provide the high wages for its workers of all grades and categories. Having estimated for these sums and allowed a percentage for profit, it can then fix its prices on the basis of its total costs—and not until then. But the goods on which those prices are fixed have to compete with goods made in countries where these first charges are infinitely lower, where the nominal *and* real wage scales are lower, and where, very often, goods for export, to compete with British manufactures, are shown some special favour by the State.

How, without the old advantage of cheap raw materials and a dominance of both the arts of manufacture and the means of transport, can Britain hope to maintain sales? She cannot hope to do so, and she is not doing so.

And in one of the main sources of income from services rendered, that of shipping, the same disadvantages are operating and thrusting her from the market, while the second main source, overseas investment, is, as we have seen, beginning to shrink.

Where on the economic seas is this change in the tide of trade driving us? Whither Britain?

It is driving us now at a quick pace towards the rocks of national bankruptcy.

Chapter III

THE PERVERSION OF PARLIAMENT

If wars were won by feasting,
Or victory by song,
Or safety found in sleeping sound,
How England would be strong!
KIPLING.

IT became possible for the British Isles to support forty-seven millions of people because they enjoyed certain natural advantages, and because the British displayed themselves as a race of hard-working technicians at home and daring adventurers abroad. The natural advantages have passed. Have the qualities of hard work and daring also passed?

In political theory the British were among the victors of the Great War. It is true that they emerged with large additions of territory under their mandatory administration, and it is true that their spokesman was one of the powerful junta which imposed peace terms on the Central Empires. But it is also true that Britain emerged from the War with her long-accumulated pool of overseas credit dissipated, and ready for the greatest disillusionment that has ever smitten a victorious race. The illusion was that the fruit of victory was to be perpetual peace for a land fit for heroes to live in. The millions of men who came back to civilian life from the fighting services found that their sacrifices and discomforts had not been for the defence of some

28

shining ideal called Britain, or for some glowing idea called democracy, but for the defence of a mass of war profiteers ranging from naturalised Jewish magnates who had done well out of munitions to Welsh miners who had actually struck work when their fellows were being butchered by incompetent military commanders in the shambles of France and Flanders. Troops who had made an allotment to their wives out of a shilling a day felt more like dupes than heroes when they met their civilian friends who had drawn high wages at constantly increasing rates in the munition factories. In the muddle of demobilisation and the unorganised scramble for jobs even the cameraderie of the trenches disappeared. If the War had been fought and endured to produce and preserve post-war Britain, the object seemed unworthy of the sacrifice and effort. It seemed even less so when in 1928 the Stock Exchange became a roaring casino, to the enrichment of rogues and the impoverishment of honest families, as a kind of wild aftermath to the politicians' failure to prevent a coal stoppage from leading to the General Strike two years earlier.

Far from the war having brought into being a new and sweeter order of society, it seemed to have intensified the worst evils of the older years.

It is, even now, not easy to assess the blow which this disillusionment dealt to the traditional patriotism of the British.

For generations the British had been taught to revere their Parliamentary system as an ideal form of Government. In one generation they discovered that it was a system which had not saved them from the holocaust of war, which could not give them a well-ordered peace, and which in a badly ordered peace could not direct their energies in such a way that their livelihoods could be counted reasonably secure from one year to another. What was far worse for the national morale, it was forced upon the national consciousness that the system not only did not render elementary social justice, but actually needed injustice for its continuance.

It was undoubtedly this realisation that accounted for the swing of the younger generations to senti-mental Socialism and to Communism, a swing of allegiance which produced eventually the famous vote of the Oxford Union against fighting for King and country. But Socialism, with its denial of rewards for enterprise and its threat of placing incompetents in command of essential services, was so alien to the ingrained tradition of the race that it could not command the imagination of those who *thought* about politics rather than *felt* about social inequity.

Disgusted with the ineptitudes and hypocrisies of the old-fashioned Parliamentary democracy as con-ducted under the party system, large bodies of young men and young women cried, "a plague on all your houses," and turned to other interests. Why should they worry and fret about politics if the end of all their mental wear and tear was only to be the return to Parliament of the same old types of caucus candidates, some as the delegates of trade unions and some as the attaches of great commercial interests and some as mere social or economic climbers. It was unfortunate for Britain that this mixture of moods came at a time when our economic development was ruining the prospects of individual enterprise. The big corporations were driving out of the competitive field the small entrepreneur, and supposedly beneficent but short-sighted legislation was making it difficult, if not impossible, for young citizens with little or no capital to start businesses of their own.

Among the rank and file of the workers the institution of labour exchanges allied to unemployment relief was killing the old principle that every man is responsible for finding his own livelihood and was confirming the much more comfortable belief that the State must tend its citizens either by finding for them acceptable work or providing the means of subsistence.

With the glory gone from war and much of the old excitement gone from peace, it was little wonder that the vicarious thrills of the cinema screen drew young people away from the more personal preoccupations of their fathers.

Boom and slump seemed beyond the wit of man to control, so why worry to be ambitious? The League of Nations and a thing called Collective Security were, together, to keep the country safe from attack, so why worry about amateur soldiering in the Territorials? Successive candidates at successive elections promised more and more free amenities from the public purse, so why worry to be personally industrious, since these things would rain down upon the active and inactive alike?

Emigration was no longer possible to ardent spirits.

Thus it was that a vast pall of apathy and lethargy wrapped the nation. "What is the use of effort?— work, and debt, and disappointment have us in a net," was the general mood, a mood baffling to those who had lived a large part of their own adult lives before the crash of 1914.

The chief symptom of this mood was—and is—a complete abandonment of the old respect for the institution of Parliament.

This contempt for Parliament was beginning to show itself in many quarters before the War of 1914, but it only became fairly general in the two decades following the Treaty of Versailles, during which it became more and more frequently demonstrated that as a machine of Government Parliament was inadequate for its functions and as a method of Government it had become perverted and therefore dangerous.

The reasons for this inadequacy and perversion are not hard to state.

Of these reasons the first is that the whole nature of Parliament has changed although its name and outward forms have not changed. The original purpose of a gathering of the Commons was to talk about taxation. In the early days of our Parliamentary institutions there was a permanent council which consisted of the important men of the State, who, with the King, debated the needs of the time and made the laws. These important men were the Nobles and Bishops. They approximated to what to-day we call the House of Lords. In addition to this Council on special occasions the voices of the Free Men and the lower Clergy were solicited, and as these two bodies were large in numbers they chose representatives to speak for them.

"On rare occasions, this expanded Council when summoned, finding itself in the presence of the Government, would talk of other things than taxation. If the State was in peril, for instance, the representatives might council a remedy. But taxation was the main object of their coming. For the twin conceptions of private property and of liberty were, in the Middle Ages, so strong that our modern idea (which is the old Roman idea) of a tax being imposed arbitrarily by the Government, and being paid without question, was abhorrent to those times. A tax, for the men of the Middle Ages, was essentially a *grant*. The Government had to go to its subjects and say: 'We need for public purposes so much; can you meet us? What can you voluntarily give us?'"*

The Commons, that is to say, met to decide how much they would allow the State from their own stores. To-day the House of Commons meets, as regards taxation, to decide how much a Chancellor of the Exchequer shall be allowed to take from the

*"The House of Commons and Monarchy," H. Belloc. 1920.

people at large. The difference of principle is vital.

· Between the accession of Henry IV in 1399 and the Reformation political events in England changed the whole character of the nation. The Free Men and the lower Clergy decreased in power and importance, and the squires and merchants became correspondingly powerful. By the time of the Stuarts the House of Commons was not only not a gathering of the true commons of England, it was not the old occasional summoning of representatives to discuss taxation. It had become a permanent institution with a special characteristic. That special characteristic was that it consisted of rich men who disputed the power of the King, and who were of a type trained in the art of Government by their normal avocations. The very word Statesman which we now apply to a professional politician who by luck or cunning has attained to a seat in the Cabinet then meant a man who owned and managed an Estate, a meaning it still bears in some remote northern counties of England.

From shortly after the Reformation until the later years of the eighteenth century the House of Commons was, in fact, but not in name, an aristocratic instrument of Government. It worked well for that very reason, because those exercising its chief functions were men of special education and training. They were men who could wilfully put the good and preservation of Britain before the need to pander to the demands or feelings of any particular class of the community. Both the Lords and Commons were, in actuality, Houses of a governing caste, in whom the masses of the people, whatever their grudges might be, had confidence, and whose authority in the day-to-day details and the broad policies of government was undisputed.

It was a very long time before the franchise came to be regarded as a right. In the very early days of the English Parliament the summons was not even regarded as a privilege. Mr. G. M. Trevelyan says of it in the days of Henry III:

> Then and for long afterwards the summons to Parliament was often regarded as a burden, grudgingly borne for the public good, much as the companion duty of serving on a jury is still regarded to-day. Communities, particularly boroughs, often neglected to send their representatives; and even the elected knights of the shire sometimes absconded to avoid service.

Perhaps the widest cut made at the older representation of the House of Commons was the Act of 1430 which deprived the general body of "freeman suitors in the Shire Court" of their franchise and limited the right of voting for knights of the shire to the forty shilling freeholders. This Act was passed to exclude all but the gentry from Parliament and had the effect of greatly increasing the power of the Nobility, with the unforeseen result that Parliament was allowed to wax strong and eventually to override the Nobility themselves.

It is our pleasant theory that the Reform Bill of 1832 made the aristocratic Commons into a democratic institution. In a work so widely read as H. G. Wells' "Outline of History" the chronological table solemnly puts against that date that "The first Reform Bill in Britain restored the democratic character of the British Parliament." The truth is that the House had never been democratic in character, and all the Reform Bill did was to extend the franchise to a few of the more trustworthy middle classes. The giving of the vote to the £10 householders and the tenant farmers, and the sweeping away of the Rotten Boroughs in favour of the new industrial townships, certainly led the way to later extensions of the franchise, but in themselves they did not alter the character of Parliament, which remained essentially the instrument of a specially educated and trained governing caste, with little responsibility to its constituents.

Throughout the prosperous and imperialistic years of the nineteenth century Britain grew rich and great not because her Parliament was democratic, but because it was not democratic. She prospered not because the will of the people prevailed, but because the will of a certain oligarchy prevailed.

By 1832 the governing caste could afford to widen the franchise, for in the eighteenth century—almost by accident, as is the English way—there had developed a system of Government which robbed the House of Commons of much of its power and significance. This system we call to-day Cabinet Government. Lest I should be suspected of prejudice in describing it I will again borrow a few sentences from G. M. Trevelyan, sentences which demand to be carefully pondered:

It is doubtful whether nobles and squires would ever have consented to concentrate such powers in the Lower House, if they had thought of it as a strictly popular body. But they thought of it as a House of gentlemen, many of them nominees or relations of the Peerage, as the "best club in London," as the "Roman Senate" to which the highest interests of the country could be safely committed.

Under these conditions the aristocratic Eighteenth Century made a great contribution of its own to the growth of British political tradition. The aristocrats devised the machinery by which the legislature could control the executive without hampering its efficiency. This machinery is the Cabinet system and the office of Prime Minister. . . . The Cabinet system is the key by which the English were able to get efficient government by a responsible and united executive, in spite of the fact that the executive was subject to the will of a debating assembly of five or six hundred men.

The British Cabinet, from the days of Walpole until the very dawn of last century, remained essentially an aristocratic body, and a small body. Huskisson, who entered the Cabinet in the 1820's, was not in the strictest sense of the word an aristocrat, nor was Peel, but both, like Gladstone who followed them, were of the moneyed class and underwent the aristocratic schooling at a great public school and Oxford University. Disraeli was, perhaps, the first genuine non-aristocrat to become Prime Minister, but even he had to assume the rôle and the status of a country gentleman, to which the Bentincks helped him.

By far the most sweeping change in the character of Parliament that occurred in the nineteenth

4

century was that inaugurated by the Act of 1884, of which R. H. Gretton* rightly and succinctly says:

> . . . the Bill swept away the old property limitations of the vote in country places, and gave it, as in the boroughs, to the occupiers of rated dwelling houses. It thus enfranchised the labourer; and the change, both in the number and in the educational level of the electorate, was great.

With this Act the dykes were down. There was still a pretence at a property qualification for the right to vote, but the way was open to later Acts that gave the vote to men and women indiscriminately. By some curious twist in the British mentality, the extension of the franchise was mixed in the mind with the idea of liberty. In 1843 Carlyle derided

> the notion that a man's liberty consists in giving his vote at election hustings, and saying, "Behold, I, too, now have my twenty-thousandth part of a Talker in our National Palaver,"

but in our time even that boast is moderate in its folly, for the voter to-day can often only claim a fifty-thousandth part in one Talker in an assembly of 615 members.

Originally the vote had been not a privilege and certainly not a right, but a function. After 1884 it became a right, and Parliament was elevated into the bulwark of the people's liberty. Those who grow hysterical about Parliamentary Democracy should examine carefully the value of the right to vote and the strength of the bulwark to their supposed liberty.

*"A Modern History of the English People."

When, every few years, generally at the choice of some "party manager," the British free man is asked to give his vote to someone who may represent him in Parliament—what actually happens? The mass of from twenty to fifty thousand voters in any one constituency is confronted by two—possibly three—candidates. These candidates are chosen not by the constituency whose suffrages they seek but by a caucus of secret persons. (How freely accepted is the fiction that a constituency chooses its own candidates and how hollow is the pretence is admirably shown in a political biography published the very day these words are written. Mr. Bechhofer Roberts, in his Life of Sir John Simon, remarks casually of his hero's entry into Parliament, "He had been offered by Herbert Gladstone, the Chief Liberal Whip, the choice of several seats—subject, as is always politely said, to the agreement of the local political committee.") Of these candidates it is rare that either is a local man or in any way associated with the locality he seeks to represent. One will probably be an adventuring lawyer, or a retired man of business, or what is colloquially known as a "carpet-bagger." The other will either be of the same kidney or he will be a trade union leader, who will not, if elected, strive to represent his electors but will devote his energies to pressing forward the sectional interests of his fellow unionists.

These candidates will have the task of presenting their views to a politically ignorant electorate—for none will deny that the large mass of voters, including as it does feather-headed "flappers" and half-educated young men and women whose abilities do not command from society in any other department of life the slightest trust or responsibility. Those views will range over a wide variety of the most complicated economic and political questions, which few of the candidates themselves will even superficially understand. As a result, on catch words and skilful propaganda the ignorant electors will cast their votes for equally ignorant members.

Most of the candidates will owe their choice as candidates to qualifications quite remote from the ability to conduct the affairs of the State. Some will be chosen because of their ability to subscribe heavily to the funds of a political party, others because of their special skill in weaving words about the popular issues of the day. All will owe their election as members to a fortuitous combination of circumstances which will not include the possession of special competency in the work of statecraft.

When all the members are elected, the House of Commons which results will have no relationship at all to the way in which the whole mass of electors has cast its votes. A Party which secures, say, one quarter of the total votes will by no means secure one quarter of the seats in the House of Commons. It may secure more; it may secure less. In one constituency of 40,000 voters a member of the Blue Party may win by securing 21,000 votes against his opponent's 19,000. In the next constituency of 40,000 members the Blue candidate may win by

securing 30,000 against his opponent's 10,000. One
has a majority of 2,000 votes, the other of 20,000.
One in the House of Commons will speak for 30,000
and the other for 19,000, but in the two constituencies together 29,000 voters will have no spokesman.

As a rough and ready method of ascertaining the
views of the nation this method, with all its electoral
accidents, may have much to be said for it, but one
thing cannot be said for it—it is not a method by
which representative government is attained, nor
would it be so even if the candidates were genuinely
chosen by the electors instead of being foisted upon
them by remote caucuses in the Capital.

Indeed, so little is genuine representative government trusted that no man or woman may come
forward as a candidate unless he or she is prepared
to deposit a sum of money to be forfeited unless
a minimum number of votes is obtained. This
deposit system is applauded as a means of keeping
the polls free from cranks and penniless adventurers,
as if—under a democratic system—cranks and adventurers without money had not as much right to
ask for votes as cranks and adventurers with money!

In Constitutional Theory the King entrusts the
Government of the country to a statesman whom he
selects for the task. This statesman gathers round
him a number of colleagues, of whom the King
approves. These form the Government, the holders
of certain Offices of State comprising the Cabinet.
The Government must submit its legislative proposals and its suggested taxes to the House of

Commons. The House debates and amends the proposals in the form of Bills, and passes them—except for money Bills—to the House of Lords. The Upper House also debates and amends, and, if necessary, passes back the amended Bill for approval. When both Houses are satisfied, the Bill goes to the King for the Royal Assent and becomes law, thereafter to be interpreted in the Courts by lawyers.

The process of debate and amendment is neither simple nor speedy. It involves, as every schoolboy knows, the procedure of drafting and then introducing the Bill, which must pass First and Second Reading, Committee and Report Stages, and Third Reading. The time devoted to its consideration and discussion is cut into by many other calls upon the time of Parliament, and the need to end debates at a particular hour.

When there is disagreement upon any point under discussion the House divides itself, and the *yeas* file patiently through one Lobby, the *nays* through another, so that they may be counted, the whole business of the House being at a standstill while this is done.

There is no distinction between kinds of business; all must occupy the time of the whole House, except when the Bill under discussion is referred to Committee. Thus some matter of local importance only to Sutherlandshire or Cornwall may hold back business vital to the whole Empire.

It will be readily realised that the machinery of

Parliament, which was evolved—if machinery can be said to evolve—over many centuries, was perfectly adequate for its purpose when the Commons consisted of men of special experience and education, elected by a small minority of similar men with a definite personal economic stake in the country, whose chief business it was to discuss what the country could afford to find in the way of funds for the purposes of the State or, occasionally, to discuss broad principles of Government. But that machinery was wholly unsuited to control by men called from quite other avocations to the full conduct of the political and economic life of the country and depending for their political existence upon the votes of great masses of people who had no knowledge of either politics or economics.

Once the scope of business in the Commons widened, and the duty of Government was no longer confined to "securing the enforcement of contracts and the preservation of law and order," the methods and procedure of Parliament were far too leisurely. As Hugh Chisholm says of early Parliaments, "it must never be forgotten that in these early times, and indeed long after, the making of new laws is as abhorrent as it is rare. The cry of the nation, so often expressed in the charters, is not for the making of a new law but for the preservation of old ones, while the levying of taxes is almost unknown except for the purposes of national defence." The attempt to apply the leisurely machinery which was shaped for such purposes to the modern lust for more and more legislation has never been successful. It has caused Parliament to fall into disrepute and has gravely hampered the material progress of the nation.

Once Parliament, designed for the use of a select and responsible governing caste, fell into the hands of demagogues it was bound to become mischievous, and its perversion was aided by the loss of its prestige caused by the payment of Members and various scandals, of which the downfall of Jabez Balfour, Horatio Bottomley and other less rogues and the Marconi case are examples. Not the least of the blights which followed the invasion of Parliament by the demagogues was the wholesale bribery of electorates with promises of public benefits. The old-fashioned bribery of an elector by a payment for his vote was an abomination, but it was an abomination that could be detected and punished. The new-fashioned method of bribing great masses of voters by promising to their class or section some benefit at the public expense is not even stamped as an abomination, so low has Parliamentary Democracy brought the public morals of the country.

To the justification of these denunciations of the system the pages of this book are devoted. But there is one denunciation even more deadly which is also to be justified by an examination of recent events. It is that not only can a country so governed not compete for the livelihood of its inhabitants with other countries whose governments are of a different kind, but that a country relying on an out-moded, inept and corrupt Parliamentary system cannot arm itself against the possible attacks of its avaricious neighbours.

Attachment to Parliamentary Democracy, which, despite popular delusion, had never any connection with popular liberty, threatens us with economic disaster and prevents our sound defence against military defeat and destruction. If we are to avoid these dooms the system must either be drastically amended or completely abandoned in favour of some other system.

With that amendment or abandonment there must come a new national mode of life, for in the follies and flaws of Parliamentarianism is to be found at once a symptom and a cause of the easy-emotionalism and refusal to face facts that make the British to-day appear decadent in a Continent where new forces are moulding other nations to a new virility. That virility we must match—or perish.

But virility is only of value if it can express itself in prompt action, and to our obsolete Parliamentary machine prompt action is not possible.

A change in the national temper and a reform of the system of Government are both essential, but neither alone can save us from the perdition to which we now race. They must be achieved together.

The first means to that double achievement is that we should see things clearly and give them their proper names, refusing to call a muddled and un-democratic system by the word "democracy" and refusing any longer to condone a national lassitude by calling it "liberty."

CHAPTER IV

THE FIASCO OF DISARMAMENT

Pale Ebenezer thought it wrong to fight,
But Roaring Bill, who killed him, thought it right.
                                        H. BELLOC.

THE first need that life lays on its creatures is that of finding the means of life. The master member is not the heart or the head, but the belly. Until that is satisfied all spiritual and cultural aspirations must wait. It is so with men; it is so with nations. An individual man, in some mood of high heroism, may prefer to perish rather than be baulked of some aspiration, but no statesman has a right to drive a nation to its doom for the sake of some aspiration which he, personally, or he and some group of adherents, may hold more dear than survival.

It is the realisation of this which must be the touch-stone of all policy.

Hatred of war, dislike of the economic waste of piled up armaments, and of the regimentation of daily life—these are emotions shared by all civilised people. But if the prevention of war is only to be found in adequate defensive arms and a disciplined community, all three emotions cannot be gratified simultaneously. Since war is only an extension of policy from the realm of negotiation to the field of force, and since sixty-five recognised "Sovereign States" must at various times find their policies clashing beyond the power of negotiation to reconcile them, war must remain an ever-present threat to humanity.

At the end of the war-to-end-war there was founded the League of Nations. Its creation was a world-wide recognition of the unpalatable fact set out in the previous paragraph. It was not an association of nations who thought war unthinkable, but of nations who thought war likely. The final sanction which it proposed to apply to any nation that transgressed its code of conduct was force. The uttermost it laid upon its members was a pledge not to make war after a quarrel until there had been a specified delay of months in which negotiations and arbitrations could be further applied.

It promised well. Many—of whom I was one—had great faith in its possibilities. It failed because the fifty or so nations who composed it refused to apply force to those who flouted it, and even refused in several cases to apply an agreed general boycott known as "economic sanctions." They refused for two main reasons—either that they sympathised with the flouter rather than the flouted or that they would not risk the destruction which the application of force would mean to their own peoples. Its failure was a demonstration that those nations realised that in our time war imperils national survival and that the first need and wish of any nation is to survive rather than to perish for an idea or an ideal.

From the viewpoint of spiritual and cultured humanity it is depressing that this should be so—but it *is* so, "and there's an end on't!"

The failure of "collective security," because many nations preferred to survive rather than risk perishing for an idea or an ideal, is only one aspect of the war risk. The other aspect is that the idea that wars cannot "pay" those who make them is quite a recent idea and is not shared by all nations.

In the history of Germany war has certainly paid. When Frederick the Great applied the doctrines of Machiavelli and made war after a broken pledge, he made possible the great nation of to-day. When Bismarck, by doctoring a telegram, forced the war of 1870, the third campaign in six years, he crowned the work of Frederick by crowning a Prussian king as German Emperor.

From the viewpoint of Christian morality the Prussian wars of the eighteenth century, including, as they did, three robberies of Poland, were indefensible. The war with Denmark in 1864, the war with Austria in 1866 and the war with France in 1870 had a justification that Frederick's campaigns lacked— they were aids to survival as well as gratifications of expansionist ambition.

Indeed, in the political philosophy of mankind before 1918 , few would have been prepared to contest the argument that expansion itself was an aid to survival. Britain least of all could dispute that contention without hypocrisy, for Britain, like Germany, had found that war certainly "paid."

It would be pleasant still to be able to credit the legend of one's school days, that Britain possessed herself of world dominion because of some divine civilising mission, but it is not true.

It will be quite obvious to anybody who thinks for a moment about the chances of history that Great Britain was by no means predestined for her present position as one of the seven major Powers of the world. She might have remained a small island kingdom, with an appropriately low population, living very much as Sweden lives. She might have been annexed by some other Power, and was, indeed, once described in the French Parliament as merely "a French colony that has turned out badly." Neither of these fates was hers. She became the Britain we know, but only by the display of considerable bellicosity and fighting qualities.

Her population, needing elbow room both for its human surplus and its products and services, made itself a world Empire. From the French were taken India and Canada, from the Dutch parts of Africa and Australasia. China at the mouth of the canon was compelled to open special treaty ports that Britons might trade in opium and other desirables. Egypt was allowed to fall into debt, and on default was virtually annexed. The neighbouring territory of the Sudan was invaded by armoured trains and Gatling guns, the natives shot down like sheep. Two rural republics in South Africa that happened to contain much gold were perpetually harassed and finally conquered after nearly four years of war.

As Britain grew in political stature Europe found that her weight was always poised ready to be thrown into the military scales against any Power that threatened to dominate that continent. During the 236 years that have passed since May 1702, the major wars in which Britain has disported herself aggregate no fewer than 102 years, without counting other wars that filled some of the intervals. They make an impressive list.

War of Succession	1702—1713	...	11 years
War with Spain	1718—1721	...	3 ,,
Spanish War	1739—1748 ⎫ ...		9 ,,
War with France	1744—1748 ⎭ ...		
Seven Years' War	1756—1763 ⎫ ...		7 ,,
War with Spain	1762—1763 ⎭ ...		
American War	1775—1782 ⎫ ...		7 ,,
War with France	1778—1783 ⎭		
War with Spain	1780—1783 ⎫ ...		5 ,,
War with Holland	1780—1783 ⎭		
Napoleonic Wars	1803—1815 ⎫ ...		12 ,,
War with America	1812—1814 ⎭		
War with Russia	1854—1856 ...		2 ,,
Boer War	1899—1902 ...		3 ,,
European War...	1914—1918 ...		4 ,,
Abyssinia	1868		1 year
Ashantee 1st, 2nd and 3rd ...	⎧1824-26, 1873-4 ⎫ ⎩1895-6, 1900 ⎭		12 years
Zululand	1879 and 1880 ...		1 year
Burmah	1824-6, 1852-3		
	1885-91 ...		3 years
Mashonaland	1896		
Sudan	1884-5, 1896-9 ...		4 ,,
Somaliland	1901 and 1904		
Transvaal	1876—1881		
In India against the French...	1746—1749 ...		3 ,,
Afghanistan	1878—1883 ...		5 ,,

(The Indian Mutiny, wars on the North-West Frontier, fighting in Palestine, must also be added.)

As the result of these many wars and the vigorous exploitation of native territories in various parts of the world Britain's power and wealth were firmly established. It was only when she emerged victorious from the War of 1914-18, with much ex-German territory under her control, that her old attitude of "what we have, we hold," ceased to be backed by a display of the necessary determination and arms to make the boast good. For the first time in British memory, warfare had been the business and calamity of the whole nation, and not the trade of a severely professional army re-inforced by a few enthusiastic volunteers. The Empire had lost a million men, and there was hardly a home which had not either felt the death or mutilation of one of the family or suffered hardship and impoverishment. Even the ancient glory had gone from war. In the discomforts and horrors of shell-churned mud there was no romance of personal combat. It was all a devil's mosaic of alternate patches of sordid monotony and ghastly agonies.

The demagogic politicians who had led the people, in the high name of democracy into the four-year Gethsemane were not popular. Their charges were restive. To satisfy the clamour there was, first, another, and ultimate, extension of the franchise, and next much talk of "open diplomacy," "no more war" and "disarmament."

Germany, held by all to be war guilty, having been stripped of her overseas possessions, although she had accepted an armistice on the assurance that no territory would be taken from her, was compelled by an un-negotiated treaty to disarm first. The assurance was that German disarmament was the first step to world disarmament. This assurance the British believed. They, too, enthusiastically disarmed.

It was not so with France and with the small States that had been carved out of the European territories of the defeated Central Empires. In a very short time after the signing of the Treaty of Versailles Germany found herself surrounded with more armaments than had encircled her before 1914. The post-treaty States had not only been placed under no obligation not to arm, they had been actively encouraged to arm. Their military strength was regarded by France as a guarantee that Germany as a military Power would not rise again from the ashes of 1918.

Quite apart from any higher motive, it suited the British Government to disarm, because the cost of armaments in the years immediately following the War, assuming that defence would have been properly tended, would have been so crippling as to make impossible the increased social services and the great housing schemes and the general reconstruction that had to be embarked upon to give colour to the promise of a land fit for heroes. The endeavour of the money powers in Britain was to avoid at all costs an unbalanced Budget and to restore Britain, as soon as possible, to her status as the great lending centre of the world. It was felt, also, that the prime necessity was to free industry from as many burdens as possible that trade might overtake the lost ground of the war years, during which the services of five million men had been withdrawn from profitable employment. Not for the first time in our history, the material need and the moral aspiration were strangely akin.

The assumption in which the people were encouraged was that, as Germany was disarmed, Russia was still in the throes of her revolution, and Europe was otherwise filled with pacific and just allies, there could no longer be any need for bloated armaments. If there should be trouble, the organisation of nearly fifty just nations at Geneva, all pledged to the exercise of "collective security," was an adequate protection.

This assumption ignored two or three facts. The allies in Europe were neither pacific nor just. They were armed and suspicious and bulging with loot taken from their neighbours.

Collective security as early as 1923 neither prevented one member of the League from bombing Corfu nor applied any punishment for the act in the way of a deterrent. Thirdly, although Germany was disarmed there was no guarantee that, filled as she was with a sense of wrong at having been tricked into an armistice and oppressed by a false treaty, she would remain unarmed while those about her increased their equipment for war. Lastly, there was no guarantee that the pacific and just allies would long remain allies.

5

These things were of no account. All that mattered was that Britain, herself heavy with the accumulated loot of more than two hundred years, was tired and, therefore, moral about war. If Britain wanted peace it was unthinkable that anyone else should want war. Militarism had been defeated and all was for the best in the best of all possible worlds.

Britain, self-bereft of the means of enforcing her will, began to hector, bully and nag those other nations to whom the world seemed not quite so perfect. This dangerous habit—dangerous because those who were affronted were themselves both proud and armed—was allowed to flourish as a direct result of one of the great weaknesses of the Parliamentary system. By telling the electorate the truth about Britain's relative military weakness the Government would have stood self-condemned as having failed in its primary duty of keeping the country safe from aggression. The truth was not only not told, but something was told which was not the truth.

Similarly, Britain, having been led into disarmament, partly from a too ingenuous belief that every nation would honour the Treaty of Versailles and partly because a "democracy" had to be given sweeping social benefits rather than defences, had to be allowed to suppose that her lack of arms was more than compensated for by the protection of "collective security."

When the League of Nations failed utterly to

prevent the first Japanese conflict with China and proved futile to prevent or stop a protracted war between two minor South American countries, a statesman who was under no necessity to keep a mass of ignorant supporters hoodwinked could have denounced the League for the failure it had become, and withdrawn from it.   This was not possible in our Parliamentary democracy because such a denunciation would have been regarded as "a betrayal of the League," which would have been construed as betraying the dead who had given their lives in the last war to achieve a League which would help to prevent future wars.

In other words, to the "democratic" statesmen of Britain the League had ceased to be a means to an end, which might fail and be replaced, and had become an end in itself.   It was no longer peace that had at all costs to be preserved.   It was the League that had to be preserved, even though circumstances had changed it from a protection to a danger.

It had so changed for one very simple reason.   In its inception the League had held out the promise that at least an overpowering majority of the nations of the world would at moments of menace unite against a single aggressor.   When the United States refused even to enter the League, and Japan and Germany having entered left it, and when Italy, though still a Member, quarrelled violently with what remained of it, this hope of unity was dead. The League had then become an uneasy alliance of the few great Powers that remained in it against those others.

Unfortunately for Britain the two other major powers in this accidental and uneasy alliance were Russia and France. Russia was avowedly and aggressively Bolshevist; France was riddled with Communism. Against Bolshevism and Communism Germany, Italy and Japan had declared an undying hatred. As a result the world took sides as Red and Anti-Red States, and Britain, anti-Red in every fibre of the national being and the chief early enemy of Bolshevism, found herself side by side with the Reds.

There was an extraordinary position—Britain, the most Imperialistic of nations, standing unarmed with half-armed France by the side of a bloody tyranny like the Soviet to rebuke and antagonise well-armed Germany, Italy and Japan for displaying Imperial ambitions. To the foreign mind her stand seemed the very triumph of hypocrisy. To the British mind it seemed like suicidal mania. Had it not been for the advent of Mr. Chamberlain as Prime Minister there can be no question that such a stand would have proved fatal. It was his determination to heal the breach between Italy and Britain and to try to restore mutual confidence between Britain and Germany that eased the growing tension to some extent and, while not removing the danger of conflict, made it less immediate.

CHAPTER V

THE TRAGEDY OF EDENISM

"I must act according to the dictates of my conscience."
By no means, my conscientious friend, unless you are quite sure that
yours is not the conscience of an ass.

RUSKIN, *Fors. Letter* 54.

WHEN the historian tries to discover how it came about that Britain from a position of supreme prestige in 1918 came so low in the years 1935-1938 he will, surely, fasten upon two reasons. Under the Premierships of Mr. Ramsay MacDonald and Mr. Stanley Baldwin the electorate was shielded from unpleasant facts about Britain's economic position, with the result that the coal stoppage and General Strike of 1926 were succeeded by the economic crisis of 1931, and in foreign affairs the electorate was shielded from unpleasant facts about Britain's military position, with the result that stronger nations whom the Britons had been led to despise were able at will to ignore and insult Great Britain when she tried to exert force in international affairs.

When the War of 1914-18 ended, the nations which engaged in it had really no justification for supposing that they could thereafter look to a higher and better standard of life. Four years of trade disruption and economic waste really meant that for many years to come those nations whose trade had been injured would have to work hard and live hard to restore it. But Great Britain with her vast and congested population had, if she was to avoid social disruption, not only to try to restore her trade but also to re-house her people and to find for them a reasonable standard of life whether they were employed or not. Having pinned her faith to what was called democracy she could not, even for their own sakes, dragoon her people to hard labour and hardship. Her financial statesmen felt compelled to lower the heavy rates of taxation which the War had imposed on industry and the individual citizen alike. Economy on arms was a godsend to them.

For fifteen years there seemed no reason why the Government should not be lavish, why £20,000,000 should not be given by the taxpayer to the coal miners to avert a general strike, even if the gift did not avert a general strike, and why unemployment benefits, housing subsidies, and the like, should not be found from the public purse without anxiety. When the world slump came in 1929, and the amount of industry and trade on which taxation was levied shrank alarmingly, it was easier for a Labour Government to continue its lavish disbursements than to tell its supporters that the country was heading for a national bankruptcy. Even when the crash of 1931 brought into existence the National Government nobody had the courage to tell the nation that it had been living too high. The whole effort was to assure the nation that new economies and hardships would be purely temporary and that very soon all cuts would be restored.

Either the statesmen were themselves deceived or they were deceiving the electorate.

There was not even an attempt by public leaders to invite the masses of the people to consider what their cherished high-standard of living meant to them, and whether more cheap foreign radio sets, bigger and better films from Hollywood, more road houses, a debauch of cheap cosmetics really meant a higher standard of life at all. Mr. Baldwin from time to time spoke movingly about the rising wood-smoke, but nothing was done to arrest the decay of the English countryside. British agriculture continued to decline and the British theatre to perish while the importers of cheap cars and tinned foods and Hollywood celluloid waxed fat.

Townships that had once flourished on British exports, like the stricken textile towns and ship-building cities of the North, were breeding parasitical and miserable communities, but what did it matter! Britain on the whole was doing quite well, and was cheered in its apparent prosperity by the thought that poor mutts in Germany and Austria and Hungary and elsewhere were struggling with adversity in the shape of waves of inflation and Communism against which the British Parliamentary democracy was so stout a protection when administered by Britons in Britain.

In their attitude towards foreign affairs in those post-war years the mass of the British public was almost entirely complacent. There was, it is true, a little bewilderment. The League of Nations

Covenant had been presented to the democracy as an
instrument that would ensure justice and peace, but
statesmen still ran about the world from conference
to conference in search of peace pacts which the
Covenant should surely have rendered unnecessary.
The names of such conferences were as many in the
Annual Registers as the place names in a poem by
Macaulay, and as pleasantly romantic. Lausanne,
Locarno, Stresa—each in turn was graced by visiting
diplomats. An American statesman achieved im-
mortality by attaching his name to the Kellogg Pact.
And at Geneva a British Labour leader and divers
colleagues struggled unsuccessfully to make a success
of a Disarmament Conference that was to implement
at last the original promise upon which the Treaty
of Versailles had been based, that a disarmed
Germany would lead the way to a world reduction
in arms.

What the people of Britain did not realise, and
they did not realise because they were not told, was
that in Europe two nations laboured under a
perpetual sense of grievance and injustice, each
having particular cause to look with envy upon
Great Britain. One was our war-time ally, Italy; the
other, Germany. Italy, a small nation, had in 1922
departed from the Parliamentary system, had begun
to re-organise and re-arm herself, and under the
leadership of Signor Mussolini had assumed an
increasingly important place in the concert of nations.
She had paid particular attention to re-armament
in the air and under the water. Germany, until

1933, was still an unarmed Power with her economic system in chaos.

In 1923 a young Austrian named Adolph Hitler had endeavoured to emulate in Germany Signor Mussolini's feat of 1922 in Italy. As Mussolini had marched on Rome and overturned the old régime which was proving inept in the face of Communism and economic disruption, so Hitler aspired to march on Berlin for a similar purpose. His *putsch* was abortive, and he was cast into prison, there to write a remarkable autobiography and brood over the wrongs of his country. But ten years later, after a strenuous and troubled career, Adolph Hitler succeeded in attaining to the Chancellorship of Germany, on January 31st, 1933.

Both Mussolini at the head of the Fascists and Hitler at the head of the Nazis had from the first turned away from the methods of democracy and had embraced the old Roman military means of organising their followers and attaining to power.

In Britain they aroused a mixture of resentment and laughter. In Great Britain a Communist agitator was tolerated as a necessary public nuisance. Occasionally one would be sent to gaol for a week or two to teach him that sedition was still a crime. That in Italy and Germany seditious persons should be treated either to doses of castor oil or to correction by physical violence aroused enormous indignation. At the same time the spectacle of grown-up men parading in uniforms and greeting each other with salutes and slogans seemed somehow childish, and the cue for merriment.   The British mind could not realise that both the force and the uniforms had been necessary to the regeneration of the countries that employed them.   The British with their relatively peaceful social history could not grasp the fact that revolutions are not to be made with kid gloves, particularly revolutions away from the brutalities of Communism.

Mr. Baldwin, to give him his due, was more alert to the needs of the governing body in Germany, for in 1936 he told the House of Commons:

> I know perfectly well how many feel about the Nazi régime. I know that there are many who regard with some disfavour a régime which lies farther East. But let us look for a moment at what is the cause of this régime in Germany, and let us, in passing, draw a lesson from it ourselves. Germany lost the War, she paid a great price in the peace treaties, and she was left with very inconsiderable armaments, and we all hoped that disarmament was coming in Europe. I need not here go into the various reasons that made those conferences fail, and how the countries of Europe lagged, but we do know that during those unhappy years which that country went through after the War she was very near to a state of revolution. The German is naturally a law-abiding man, and he had a glimpse into the abyss when Communism in Germany raised its head—and Communism was a creed of violence and force. It was beaten ultimately by another creed of violence and force, and you have that great people who during many years have seen the régime that *would* and the régime that *did* found itself on force, and what wonder that the idea of force—not an alien idea to the Teuton—should seem to dominate very much that mentality to-day.

The real significance of the triumph of Herr Hitler in Germany was, of course, that a Germany which resentfully assented to the Treaty of Versailles had given place to a Germany which repudiated that Treaty. Resentment was about to become active.

The Nazi party repudiated the charge that the guilt for 1914 lay upon Germany. They felt, and felt bitterly, that they had been tricked into the armistice by the protestations of President Wilson and British statesmen that the war was not being waged against the German people, but only against the German Junkers and that no territorial aggrandisement was sought by the Allies. This meant that they felt they had a moral right to the ex-German Colonies which had thus been taken from them by a pretence. They also felt that to deny Germany the right to arm while her neighbours were encouraged to arm was a rank injustice.

There were at that time two sane roles for Britain to assume. She could have intimated to Herr Hitler and the world that she sympathised with the German grievances, and taken steps through Geneva to redress them, or she could have ignored the German claims and prepared to protect the existing state of affairs by herself rapidly rearming, so that her wishes abroad would carry weight. She did neither of these things.

Unarmed, she chose to scold the nations who were suffering, rightly or wrongly, from a sense of injustice and grievance for behaving exactly as Britain herself had for three hundred years behaved. She had neither moral nor physical force behind her.

The consequence was that from her pinnacle of 1918 she fell to her low prestige of 1938.

In the period of that decline many statesmen held office in Britain, and to none can all the blame be imputed. But history must certainly single out one man's name as the symbol of the worst and swiftest years of our national descent—that already almost forgotten name, Anthony Eden.

Mr. Anthony Eden is no longer Foreign Secretary. We are free to ask—as so many hard-thinking people always asked—was his the most disastrous appointment ever made in public life?

His career was spectacular. To many he was a young man of unusual charm, palpable sincerity and high moral purpose. But career, charm, sincerity and high moral purpose matter nothing when weighed with achievement. It is not the man or a particular view of the man that matters. It is his record. Whatever his intentions may have been these are the things he achieved when he was potent in British foreign policy:

> He converted the ancient friendship which Italy felt for Britain and Britain for Italy into open enmity.
>
> He caused the returning amity between Britain and Germany to turn to impatience and suspicion.
>
> He permitted Britain's former ally, Japan, to pass from a mood of extreme dissatisfaction with Britain to a mood of open bellicose contempt.
>
> Knowing Britain to be relatively unarmed, and knowing that the League of Nations was no longer the all-inclusive

association which alone could take effective action, he forced sanctions against Italy, and thus exposed to the well-armed and hungry nations of the world his own nation's complete inability to back his brave words by action. He showed that "collective security," in which he commanded his own and other nations which trusted him to believe, to be a hollow sham.

By these achievements Mr. Eden reduced Britain's prestige to a lower level than it had reached since the Dutch sailed up the Medway.

His intentions may have been excellent; his achievement was deadly.

The extraordinary aspect of Mr. Eden's work in reducing to international impotence the Parliamentary Democracy of Great Britain was that it was done in the very name of Democracy—although democracy was represented by the barbaric slave-traders of Abyssinia, the plundering brigands of China and the ruthless thugs and gunmen of Red Spain. It was done in the name of democracy, although Mr. Eden's leading co-adjutor was a Jew named Finklestein who, under the *nom de guerre* of Litvinof, represented Russia's most brutal tyranny. His friendship with Russia's foreign minister was the more unfortunate for Britain because his fanatical reliance upon the truncated League had already, as has been said, linked Britain in a false and uneasy alliance with the Communists of Russia and France, although the British had no temperamental affinity with either.

The effects of Mr. Eden's false moves in permitting

such an alliance to come into being were far reaching. The regeneration and re-arming of both Italy and Germany had their origin in the determination of the leaders of those nations to destroy Bolshevism. From their viewpoint such determination might have been expected to command the sympathy, if not the active aid, of Britain, for it was the British Empire which was the object of the most venomous hatred of Moscow. For a decade after the murder of the Tzar by the Bolshevists Britain was perpetually struggling against Bolshevist propaganda and intrigue in her own cities and workshops.

Until 1934 the animosity of Russia to Britain included animosity to the League of Nations. In that year Russia joined the League, and Mr. Eden gave her welcome. "His Majesty's Government," he said, "associate themselves with a step which will effectually assist to universalise the League by including the Soviet Union within its ranks. His Majesty's Government in the United Kingdom cordially welcome the addition of so powerful a State." Far from this entry helping, as Mr. Eden thought, to "universalise" the League it was the prelude to a succession of splits from the League. By the following year the only major Powers that remained were Britain, France and the new Red recruit.

This unnatural association, and Mr. Eden's frankness in letting it be known that he preferred the atmosphere of Moscow to that of Berlin, affronted those well-armed nations which had best reason to detest, because they had best reason to know, Bolshevism. This, in turn, had a singular and sinister effect upon Britain's safety and prestige.

Between 1934 and 1937 Mr. Eden's Genevan policy achieved the almost incredible feat of depriving the British of their old security along their essential water-way to the East. In 1934 Britain still commanded the Mediterranean Sea, the Suez Canal and the Red Sea. By 1937 an unfriendly Italy menaced that command in the Eastern Mediterranean, an antagonist Fascist Spain fretted it in the West, an unfriendly Egypt stood at the North of the Suez Canal, a restless combination of Arabs and Italians threatened the Red Sea front, and victorious Italy in Abyssinia menaced the Sudan and the headwaters of the Nile.

Never was a strategical position so quickly or so needlessly reversed by the blundering of a single Minister.

As if to emphasise the impotence to which his policy had reduced Great Britain, Mr. Eden became responsible in those few years for a positive stream of notes, protests, and interrogations most of which were either received in contemptuous silence or given replies almost equally contemptuous. Before the advent of Mr. Eden at the Foreign Office a protest or communication from His Majesty's Government was neither ignored nor treated with diplomatic raillery. Under his direction so low did we sink that even General Franco, whose belligerent status Mr. Eden refused to recognise, could, with impunity, follow the example of Germany and leave unanswered British communications sent with a request for an early reply. General Franco even followed the example of Japan, which had attacked at will British ships and posts, well knowing that the most grudging and meagre "explanation" would satisfy a Parliamentary Government and an impotent Foreign Office that had no physical force with which to back its demands for satisfaction.

These ill results came from one cause. Mr. Eden, as Minister for League Affairs and later as Foreign Secretary, either would not or could not accept the twin facts that:

> His own nation had disarmed while Europe was arming.
> The League, lacking the newly-armed great Powers in Europe and the United States and Japan, was unable to speak with authority to any nation which felt angry and strong enough to defy or deride it.

Mr. Eden, in short, was not governed by things as they were, but by things as he thought they ought to be in a highly moral world. He made his wish and not the facts father to his political thought. Knowing his nation to be weak he was truculent to nations he knew to be strong, relying upon "collective security" to protect him. And of what did this "collective security" consist? It consisted of a medley of small nations of no military or economic power huddled behind a Russia in the throes of a political purge and a France in the throes of economic disruption.

There must be coupled with the name of Mr. Eden

in assigning responsibility for Britain's abrupt loss of power and prestige the names of those sentimentalists who, at the Albert Hall and elsewhere, cheered on his folly, of whom the Archbishop of Canterbury was one of the most eminent, and of those newspapers which refused to tell the truth, as they must or ought to have known it, about the relative strengths of the opposing European forces.

It may be argued in Mr. Eden's favour that he was the victim of the ignorance of his leader, Mr. Baldwin, who in May, 1935, had to confess to the House of Commons that on the question of German re-arming he had been hopelessly misinformed. He said:

> . . . I was completely wrong. I tell the House so frankly because neither I nor any advisers from whom we could get accurate information had any idea of the exact rate at which production could be, and actually was being, speeded up in Germany in the six months between November and now. We were completely misled on that subject.

There was no excuse for being so misled. In November, 1933, M. Mandel told the French Chamber of Deputies that Germany was in a position to turn out 2,500 machines each month. In March, 1935, Mr. Baldwin himself said that the British air force was only fifth in the scale of powers, and drew from Sir Austen Chamberlain, an ex-Foreign Minister, the expression of his belief that our position was even lower, and that we were probably sixth or seventh in the scale. Mr. Eden, moving freely among the most knowledgeable of Continental statesmen, should

6

have been under no illusion, and should have left his leader under none. In any event, knowing Britain to be at best only fifth in the scale of air Powers, that Minister was surely foolhardy who thrust her into the forefront of a series of acrimonious disputes where her words could only be regarded as vain vapourings and not as serious warnings of action to follow.   This was exactly what Mr. Eden did, and the legacy of his policy is such that even in June, 1938 Sir Ernest J. P. Benn could write ruefully:

> . . . we now find all the fervour recently applied to the cause of disarmament switched over to demands which taken together amount to a proposal that we should undertake war against Franco, Hitler, Mussolini and the Mikado all at one and the same time.*

However the responsibility be allotted for British policy, its results remain beyond dispute.   There remains, too, the vital question—can Britain, whose crowded islands depend for their existence upon the trading friendship of the world, whose people, in the days of aeroplanes, are the most vulnerable in the world, afford to pursue any policy which leads to enmity among those able to hurt her irreparably both in the military and economic spheres?

That is the most cynical way of stating Britain's problem.   But quite apart from the stark need of self-preservation, is there any real justification for the enmity which has been aroused? When world facts and relations are viewed without any colouring prejudice, and considered apart from the emotions

*"Debt," by Ernest J. P. Benn.

aroused by one-sided propaganda, is it possible that
the role which Britain was compelled to play until
Mr. Chamberlain's advent to power was not only
wrong-headed but wrong-hearted?

It is, at least, the duty of every Briton to search
anxiously and sincerely for the right answer to that
question, and the answer can only be found by
reviewing, without heat, the events which have led
us to our present situation.

Chapter VI

THE INSANITY OF SANCTIONS

Philanthropists may easily imagine that there is a skilful method of disarming and overcoming an enemy without causing great bloodshed, and that this is the proper tendency of the Art of War. However plausible this may appear, it is still an error which must be extirpated; for in such dangerous things as war, the errors which proceed from a spirit of benevolence are the worst. VON CLAUSEWITZ, *On War*, Book 1.

THERE are two views about the first and essential duty of a Government. One is that it must, at all costs, strive to keep the country it governs safe and prosperous. The other is that it must strive, even to the detriment of its own people, to enforce its own particular morality upon the world at large. This difference could be more unkindly expressed by saying that some people think the duty of a Government is to mind its own business, others that its duty is to meddle in everybody's business. But both will agree that to do either duty successfully the Government must first be strong, morally strong and physically strong.

In the years 1934-35 Britain, in a mood of exhaltation, aspired to be the moral mentor of the world. The occasion of this aspiration was the punitive attack by Italy upon the Abyssinians. The instrument was the League of Nations.

It would be foolish and useless to deny that at the time the great bulk of the British people believed that the aspiration was right, the Italian attack was wrong, and the instrument was sound. The Italian people believed that the aspiration was a piece of rank hypocrisy, the Italian attack was right, and the instrument was despicable.

To discover how these opposite views could be sincerely held it is necessary to retell, however familiar the story may be, the history of Britain and Italy in Africa.

Italy first effected a footing in Africa during the international scramble for territory there which filled a large part of the nineteenth century. Britain was busy at the same time acquiring, by armed penetration and aggression, Egypt, the Sudan, South Africa and the two Rhodesias. Italy's acquisition was by a purchase of land (now known as Eritrea) from the local Sultan in 1689 and a lease from the Sultan of Zanzibar of land which became known as Italian Somaliland.

As a neighbour in Africa Italy was regarded by Britain as a friendly power, and when in 1895 the Jameson Raid into the Boer Republic of the Transvaal brought Britain much odium in Europe, Italy's presence at Assowa, on the Red Sea, was particularly welcome, for Germany had invited France to co-operate in limiting "the insatiable appetite" of Great Britain.

In 1889 a treaty had made the King of Italy the intermediary for Abyssinia's relations with foreign powers. In 1891 an Anglo-Italian Pact recognised that country as an Italian sphere of influence, although France, then engaged in a tariff war with Italy, withheld such recognition.

Italy and Britain, it will be realised, were working in close amity in Africa. The year 1896 was pregnant with danger for both. Britain, following the Jameson Raid, had drawn on herself the open hostility of Germany and France. The Ministry of Lord Salisbury was also under the necessity of preparing to reconquer the Sudan. The British had thus severe pre-occupations in Africa. At that time the Emperor Menelek of Abyssinia grew angry at Italy's possessing a protectorate over the Somali coast. He accused Italy of tampering with his rebel vassals, and compelled an Italian garrison to surrender. He then made overtures for peace on terms which Italy found unsatisfactory. The Italian General, Baratieri, rejected these advances and attacked the Abyssinian force of 100,000 men at Adowa with an Italian army of only 14,500. He was completely defeated. Many of the prisoners taken by the Abyssinian tribesmen were held for over a year and subjected to horrible mutilations, the story of which still chills the Italian memory.

As a result of this debacle Italy was forced to sign a treaty recognising the independence of Abyssinia. Her loss of the protectorate was the more bitter because Britain, France, Germany and Portugal had all done well out of the partition of Africa. Even Belgium had the Congo. The loss of her protectorate naturally left Italy with exactly the feelings that Britain had had when Gordon was murdered in the Sudan, not a great many miles away. But whereas the British had sent an expedition, with the grim visaged

Kitchener at its head, and had destroyed the Mahdi, Italy took no such action. Britain, in fact, had done more than avenge the slaughter of Gordon at Khartum. She had sent about his business a French commander who had marched across Africa to Fashoda, brooking no question of her possession whether from Frenchmen or Fuzzy-wuzzy. Italy was more patient, and waited for a generation until both French and British had made economic headway in the very land where Italian troops had been slain and tortured.

Throughout the years that followed the Italo-British amity was unimpaired, and Britain continued to recognise Abyssinia as an Italian sphere of influence.

When the war of 1914 broke out Italy, in its second year, severed herself from the Triple Alliance and joined the Allies. Her change of allegiance was not disinterested, and there was no reason why it should have been. She joined the Allies on certain specific promises, all of which were solemnly engrossed in the Treaty of London. Of that Treaty Article XIII promised that:

> In the event of France and Great Britain increasing their colonial territories in Africa at the expense of Germany, these two Powers agree in principle that Italy may claim some equitable compensation, particularly as regards the settlement in her favour of the questions relative to the frontiers of the Italian colonies of Eritrea, Somaliland and Libya.

There are two queer aspects of this Article. One is that Britain, whose pride and boast it was that she

sought no territorial aggrandisement from the War,
should have contemplated as early as 1915 taking
possessions in Africa from Germany. The other is
that having made such a promise in the early days of
the year she should in the final settlement have
broken it.

Both France and Britain benefited in African
territory at the expense of Germany, but Italy—to
use a word that is ugly but right—was "bilked."
It is no explanation of that bilking that the possessions taken from Germany were called Mandated
Territories and not Colonial possessions.

This breach of faith over the Treaty of London was
not to be the last of Italy's grievances about
Abyssinia.   On December 14th and 20th, 1925, the
Baldwin Government in Britain exchanged notes with
Italy.   By this exchange of notes Britain promised
that, in return for Italian support in obtaining from
the Abyssinians a concession to build a barrage on
Lake Tana and a motor road from the Sudan to that
lake, Britain would support an Italian request for a
railway from Eritrea to Somaliland to the West of
Abyssinia's capital and would "support with the
Abyssinian Government all Italian requests for
economic concessions" in the zone covered by that
railway.

In the light of after events the result of this exchange of notes was not without humour. Abyssinia
protested to both Britain and Italy, saying to
Britain, "we should never have suspected that the
British Government would come to an agreement

with another Government regarding *our* lake!"
She then referred the matter to the League of
Nations, to which she had been admitted in September, 1923, despite Britain's opposition based on
the belief that Abyssinia was unable to fulfil her
obligations.

In 1928 the then Regent of Abyssinia, later to
become the Negus, signed a Pact of twenty years'
friendship with Italy, both Governments agreeing
not to have recourse to armed force. Despite this
agreement Italy was subject to armed force by the
Abyssinians. In the winter of 1934 the Italian
consulate at Gondar was attacked. For this un-
provoked assault the Italian Government demanded
and received both apology and reparation, as Britain
had done for Abyssinian raids and assaults in the
Sudan two years previously. But within a very few
weeks a much more serious incident occurred at
Wal-wal.

With the Wal-wal incident began the Italo-
Abyssinian episode in which Britain was to play so
strange and ignominious a part. As that incident
progressed the British public was led, or allowed, to
picture the Abyssinians as a peaceful, inoffensive
people brutally attacked by an avaricious European
Power. No picture could have been further from the
truth. It was the European Power which had been
attacked and had its nationals assaulted and its flag
insulted by armed men, the subjects of a ruler who
had pledged himself not to use armed force against
Italy. Abyssinia was a hot-bed of slavery and a

cockpit of racial and religious quarrels between barbaric tribes, and the Negus—as Britain had well
foreseen—was utterly unable to fulfil his obligations.

When the Sudanese had outraged Britain Sir
Herbert Kitchener had mown down some 10,000
dervishes with machine guns at Omdurman. Italy
did not follow that relatively recent example. She
had twice, from her viewpoint, been cheated on
British promises about territory in Abyssinia—for
that is what "adjusted frontiers" means—and economic concessions in that country. She had without
protest from Britain demanded and received reparation and apology for the Gondar incident. She had,
in concert with Britain, skilfully evaded an appeal
to the League by Abyssinia when London and Rome
had contemplated incursions into the territory
surrounding what the Abyssinians called "our lake."
In bringing Abyssinia into the League she had found
Britain indignant at the admission of so savage a
race into so responsible a body. Finally when the
Wal-wal incident occurred Italian statesmen, including Signor Mussolini, had met British statesmen
at Stresa and no word had come from them that
Britain would object to punitive action following the
assault at Wal-wal, as action had followed the
assault at Gondar.

With all this in mind, the Italians would naturally
expect from Britain sympathy, if not approval, in
their Abyssinian trouble, when the matter was
considered—as it *was* considered—at Geneva by the
League of Nations. The Italian representative might

well have expected Mr. Eden, for example, to say
to him:

> The fiendish outrages upon your troops after the slaughter
> of your army at Adowa are not only unavenged, but have
> been followed through thirty years by other outrages.
> Our own promises to you of favourable adjustments in
> Abyssinia have not been kept. Through the past thirty
> years we, at least, have always recognised your special
> position in regard to Abyssinia and have more than once
> solicited your aid or taken diplomatic advantage of your
> presence in that area. Remembering our own unrestrained
> wrath at Omdurman we must admire your military restraint.
> Remembering the very recent precedent of Gondar and our
> own action when the savage Abyssinians came raiding into
> the Sudan two years ago, we cannot now object to your
> demanding redress for the attack on your nationals at
> Wal-wal. Your action in Abyssinia is, therefore, no diplo-
> matic concern of ours. Had it been so our Prime Minister
> would have told Il Duce so at Stresa.

Imagine, then, Italy's sense of betrayal when
instead of such a statement she found the British
representative saying, in effect:

> Whatever your grievances, whatever your wrongs,
> whatever your pride of race, you must consent to sit as an
> equal with the dark Ethiopian who has wronged you. You
> must consent to have your cause judged by a medley of
> small nations under the leadership of Bolshevist Russia,
> who hates you, and Leftist France, which detests you. As
> for us—we who bilked you about Abyssinia in the Treaty of
> London and once had a very quick way with dervishes, we
> shall assume the role of the world's moral mentor, at your
> expense.

Having encountered a Britain in this mood, so
different from any expectation, Italy naturally

assumed that there was a reason for it. That reason, they quite forgivably supposed, was British jealousy of the Fascist State.

The Italian construction had an echo in many British breasts. Many people in Great Britain thought it desirable that the two great so-called "Democracies of the West," Britain and France, should show to the armed and arrogant Fascist States that collectively the non-Fascist States were their masters, and could, even without the use of military force, dominate international conduct. Mr. Eden's speeches lend colour to the belief that he, himself, cherished this view. In other words, the power of the League of Nations had to be demonstrated, Italy was arbitrarily chosen to be the object lesson, since Germany was too near and dangerous and Japan too far away and dangerous, and Britain was to be the leader of the new holy war.

If such was, indeed, the intention of the British representative at Geneva, its failure was lamentable. The result of the Geneva policy was to show exactly the opposite of what it was intended to demonstrate, for it was to show that economic sanctions were unworkable and powerless, and that not the League but the Totalitarian States were the dominators of international conduct.

For the arrant failure of the League to fulfil the work which it was supposed to do Britain has to bear a special responsibility. It was her representative, Mr. Eden, who pressed forward the application of sanctions against Italy. France displayed no great enthusiasm, and before some of the smaller States were prepared to participate it became necessary for Britain to guarantee to protect them against loss. It is not too hard a phrase to say that for the support of several of the smaller States the British delegation at Geneva had to tout and bribe in a manner ill-befitting the dignity of a great Power alleging itself to be actuated by a high moral motive.

The Article of the Covenant under which Sanctions were applied, Article 16, has four clauses, of which the two first are the most potent. They read:

> (1) Should any Member of the League resort to war in disregard of its covenants under Articles 12, 13 or 15, it shall *ipso facto* be deemed to have committed an act of war against all other Members of the League, which hereby undertake immediately to subject it to the severence of all trade or financial relations, the prohibition of all intercourse between their nations and the nationals of the covenant-breaking State and the nationals of any other State, whether a Member of the League or not.

> (2) It shall be the duty of the Council in such case to recommend to the several Governments concerned what effective military, naval, or air force the Members of the League shall severally contribute to protect the covenants of the League.

The first clause, it must be obvious, could only be effective if the "severance of all trade or financial relations, the prohibition of all intercourse" was complete. It could not be complete without the participation of the United States, Germany and Japan *unless* Britain, France, Russia and the smaller fry were prepared, in the words of the clause, to

"prevent all financial, commercial or personal intercourse between the nationals of the covenant-
breaking State and the nationals of any other State,
whether a Member of the League or not." In other
words, the sanctions authorised and envisaged by
Article 16 must in 1935 have meant not only
hostilities, or the risk of hostilities, against Italy, but
also against the United States, Germany and Japan.

It is an accepted rule in business, in parenthood
or in schoolmastering that one should never utter a
threat that one is not prepared to carry out. That
rule is even more vital in international relationships.
But Britain in 1935 was invoking Article 16 well
knowing that she had no intention of pressing it to
its conclusion and that, had she harboured such an
intention, she could not successfully achieve it.

Having led the Genevan nations to the invocation
of sanctions, Mr. Eden failed to face the implication
of his action, which was that:

> the severance of economic relations must be complete both
> in the sense of all commodities being withheld from Italy
> and the sense that nobody anywhere must be allowed to
> trade with her;
>   military sanctions had to be envisaged in addition to
> economic sanctions.

Unless these things could be assured, Italy could
successfully defy the League and expose its impotence to the world, as she had done years before
over the bombing of Corfu and as Japan had done
in the Far East.

There was, too, the very real danger that the

attempt to cripple Italy by the imposition of partial sanctions would lead to war, that that well-armed nation might retaliate to a negative attack by a positive attack. Since to the Italian mind the imposition of sanctions meant not a moral attempt to prevent war but a selfish attempt to "down" Fascism, any warlike action by Italy would in such circumstances be almost certain to have the support —either passive or active—of Germany, for Nazi Germany could not permit Fascist Italy to be ruined by a motley collection of small States led by the two Western democracies in alliance with Bolshevist Russia.

The British Government, of which Mr. Eden was the international personification, realised this danger. Britain was the dominant power in the Mediterranean. She could, in theory, make impossible the passage of other nations' ships to the Middle East by naval action. She could, in theory, close the Suez Canal. If she applied either of these measures the Italian contingents engaged in the Abyssinian adventure would be cut off from their homeland. Italy's line of communication would be severed. All would be over. Against such a contingency Italy would fight to the last shell and the last man.

Realising this, the British fleet went hot-foot to the harbour of Alexandria.

But Italy had a thousand 'planes and over eighty ocean-going submarines in the Eastern Mediterranean. The British fleet was extremely vulnerable. Almost the first thing that had to be done was to

clear away some of the "top-hamper" from our battleships to enable anti-aircraft guns to have a clear
field of fire.

The better equipped these ships were to deal with
enemy 'planes, the worse equipped they were to
perform their naval function.

To make matters worse, disarmed Britain had been
unable to supply her battleships with sufficient
ammunition to conduct any engagement lasting for
more than perhaps half an hour.   Her crews had
had to be reinforced by reservists, hustled off from
the celebration of King George's Jubilee to spend
anxious days in floating ovens of ships that had never
been designed for use in so narrow a sea.

The Suez could not be closed, for that would have
brought many enemies about Britain's ears.   The
free navigation of the Canal had been guaranteed
by the Convention between Great Britain, Austria-
Hungary, France, Germany, Italy, the Netherlands,
Russia, Spain and Turkey.   This Convention, signed
at Constantinople on October 29th, 1888, laid down
in its first Article that:

> The Suez Maritime Canal shall always be free and open,
> in time of war as in time of peace, to all merchant or war
> vessels without flag discrimination.
>
> Consequently, the High Contracting Parties agree in no
> way to prevent the free use of the Canal in time of war as
> in time of peace.
>
> The Canal shall never be used for the exercise of the right
> of blockade.

The result of the moving of the fleet to the Mediterranean was not to imperil Italy, but to jeopardise the

fleet. Politicians in London talked of closing the Canal, but Italy and the whole world knew that this would not be done.

It very quickly became equally obvious that the partial Sanctions which the League was persuaded to apply to Italy were useless for the purpose of turning her from her task in Abyssinia. They were useless just because they were partial—and partial in two senses, that only a few selected nations applied them and that not all commodities useful to Italy in war were affected.

Perhaps the most severe critic of Mr. Eden's sanction policy was Mr. Eden. The brave words of Anthony Eden, drunk with enthusiasm for Geneva, in 1935, differed greatly from the words of Anthony Eden, sobered by experience in 1937, when he told the House of Commons that:

> . . . there are two possible forms of sanctions, the ineffective which are not worth putting on, and the effective which mean the risk, if not the certainty, of war.*

This elementary truism he should have realised on September 26th, 1935, when he was first threatening Sanctions. There can be no question of his leadership in this matter, for on September 8th in that year he was joined at Geneva by Sir Samuel Hoare, the then Foreign Secretary, who opened the meeting of the Assembly with a speech that specifically endorsed Mr. Eden's lead to the Council and later on the radio told the British public how impressed he had been by the way all nations represented at Geneva were looking to Britain for advice and guidance.

7

The advice and guidance they received did not deter Italy, but did lead the world to the very brink of a new war.

How near to war Britain was leading her own nationals one man certainly realised. He was the Prime Minister, Mr. Baldwin. The very day the Italian campaign opened the Premier told his supporters at Bournemouth that it was useless for Great Britain to accept obligations under the Covenant unless she could command forces adequate to the carrying out of those obligations in case of need. He admitted that from the world at large there had reached him doubts and questionings of Britain's ability so to fulfil her obligations, and that while these doubts existed Britain's word would not carry that weight in international councils that it always had carried and ought to carry.

This—from the Minister primarily responsible for Britain's unarmed state—was a grave admission, but it did not check Mr. Eden's zeal for dangerous Sanctions, although he himself admitted in turn, in the House of Commons on October 22nd, 1935, that there had been no discussions at Geneva of military sanctions as the condition precedent of such action, collective agreement, was missing.

Quite apart from any speech making by Mr. Baldwin there was one sure sign that Mr. Eden's Government at home was apprehensive that his enthusiasm at Geneva might lead to war. Britain had to ask France if, in the event of the British Mediterranean Fleet being attacked, her ships might be permitted to put into French ports. France, on October 4th, 1935, replied with the necessary permission on condition that Britain gave a reciprocal guarantee for the future.

It should be remarked that this incident further strengthened the accidental attachment of Britain to Soviet Russia, the avowed and open moral enemy of both Italy and Germany. France, tied to Moscow by the Franco-Soviet pact, was providing shelter to British ships of war which anticipated conflict with Italy. It was not part of Britain's foreign policy to link the country's destiny to that of the Russian Bolshevists, but Mr. Eden's headstrong infatuation for the truncated League of Nations was forging link after link between the two. Each link intensified the suspicion and enmity of Rome and Berlin.

Why did Mr. Eden, with the assent of his Government, lead Britain into this thoroughly false position, a position which was to endanger the peace of the world for years to come? It is not enough to say that he thought he was doing right, for he must have known how unarmed Britain was for the responsibility with which he was shouldering her. The kindest explanation is that he had miscalculated the economic strength of the Totalitarian State and he had miscalculated the probable duration of an Abyssinian campaign.

In the second miscalculation he was in good company. So-called expert military opinion in several countries was hopelessly wrong about the probable length of such a campaign. In the

September of 1935 the *New Statesman* in a widely read and much quoted pamphlet said:

> The duration of the war is reckoned by Italian military experts at two years: by most foreign experts at at least four years, followed by guerrilla fighting for an indefinite period.

To say that he shared a misconception with others is no excuse for the British Minister's lack of shrewdness.   In the July of that year I, an amateur soldier with some little experience of mechanised warfare in mountainous country, published an article forecasting the end of the war for March or April the following year.   The campaign actually ended in a decisive victory for Italy in May.   The newspapers associated with Lord Rothermere had from the first insisted that sanctions were madness and that Italy with her modern mechanised forces must make short work of any Abyssinian resistance.   But the general impression shared by Mr. Eden was that the campaign must drag on and that Italy—in the easy slang of the day—had bitten off more than she could chew.

It was difficult then to see how such a view could prevail; it is more difficult now.   The Abyssinian warriors, as Mr. Eden must have known, were primitive tribesmen.   Even the Royal Bodyguard marched barefooted.   Modern arms were not plentiful.   They were not plentiful because the Negus feared to permit them to tribes of doubtful allegiance and because an arms embargo, of which Mr. Eden had been a supporter, allowed no free flow of supplies. Abyssinia, in any event, was not a united military nation, but a medley of undisciplined and often rebellious barbarians. Italy, on the contrary, *was* a united nation, an enthusiastic people. She was equipped with all the latest designs of tanks, 'planes, armoured cars, and field engineering facilities. To expect the tribesmen and pastoral dwellers of Ethiopia to stand long against such arms wielded by such antagonists was palpable folly. One favourite contention was that of all countries, Ethiopia was the most difficult to subdue from the air, since the inhabitants had their abodes under the rims of high peaks. To anyone who had studied aeroplanes in action such a contention was ludicrous. The destructive power of the modern bombing 'plane is such that not only the terror-stricken primitive peoples of Abyssinia but their grazing herds, their essential food supply, were at the mercy of skilled and daring pilots.

To the relatively ignorant masses of Mr. Eden's fellow countrymen it seemed incredible that Britain, the great naval Power, could fail to intimidate Italy. This feeling of invincibility was nurtured by Press cartoons and articles deriding the Duce and his arms. The masses were also led to believe that Italian tanks and troops were shortly to be defeated by an act of God, who was to send down the dreaded Abyssinian rains and engulf them in mud. But Mr. Eden, as a Member of the Cabinet, must have known how precarious was the fleet in the Mediterranean with its shortage of ammunition under the threat of 1,000 'planes and 80 submarines. He must have known how vulnerable were the ports of Britain, and the lives of forty-seven million citizens dependent on those ports for food, should a combination of air Powers be goaded to attack them. It was the current fashion of those who, lacking knowledge, supported his policy to declare that he had "called the Dictator's bluff," but as events proved, if there were any bluff, it was not by Italy. She had the cards. The bluff that was ultimately called was that of an unarmed Britain backed by a half-hearted League of Nations, quite powerless to enforce its will.

All this is clear enough now, three and more years after the event. But in 1935 Mr. Eden did not lack enthusiastic supporters. A "peace ballot" organised by the League of Nations Union, and approved by His Grace the Archbishop of Canterbury, found 11,000,000 zealots for the League. Sentimentalists of all parties found something to approve in the Government's policy, and Mr. Baldwin, always an astute tactician, found the moment opportune to appeal to the country. His reasoning was, no doubt, simple. The 11,000,000 peace balloters might be expected to vote for a Government that was sacrificing everything to the League. Sanctions had not yet hit British trade very badly. The betrayal of India to the extremists, *which robbed many hundreds of thousands of Lancashire workers of their future livelihood,* was complete and no longer a matter of dispute. A policy of re-armament had been belatedly entered upon. There was, in short, something for everybody. But standing up to the dictators was

the really popular line which the Government took
to the country.

The election resulted in the return of the National
Government. It was true that the Opposition had
cast for it 80 per cent. of the number of votes cast
for the Government, but by a familiar electoral
mischance it only secured less than 40 per cent. of
the seats. But the Government was back, with its
policy endorsed. It was a triumph for Mr. Anthony
Eden.

Russia was to enter into a new era of purges and
the shooting of generals; France was to plunge
deeper into the mire of economic disruption; Britain
was to proceed very leisurely with a programme of
re-armament, a programme so leisurely that three
years later Parliament was to be rent by a dispute
arising from our lack of air raid precautions. But
Mr. Eden had a mandate to continue, in the company
of Bolshevist Russia and Half-Communist France,
the policy of angering, antagonising and provoking
the well-armed States, which preferred some other
system of Government, while he remained completely
powerless to stay them in their courses.

Chapter VII

THE HOARE-LAVAL INCIDENT

To preserve the peace of the world is the leading object of the policy of England. For this purpose it is necessary in the first place to prevent to the utmost of our power the breaking out of new quarrels; in the second place, to compose, where it can be done by friendly mediation, existing differences; thirdly, where this is hopeless, to narrow as much as possible their range; and fourthly to maintain for ourselves an imperturbable neutrality in all cases where nothing occurs to affect injuriously our interests or our honour.

GEORGE CANNING.

THE reluctance of British statesmen to face unpleasant realities was, perhaps, never better displayed than in the programme upon which Mr. Baldwin appealed to the country on October 27th, 1935. The truncated League of Nations was showing that partial Sanctions could not deter Italy in Abyssinia, the long effort to achieve international disarmament was palpably futile, for in Italy, Japan and Germany arms were being piled up and the post-Treaty States which had from the first heavily armed themselves were not disposed to disarm. But the Government of Britain announced that the keystone of its foreign policy was still the League, that gaps in Britain's defences would be repaired in the next few years and that at the same time efforts would not be spared to bring about a general limitation of armaments.

When the new Parliament met the official antagonism to Italy was not abated, but by the time the King's Speech was in progress it was generally realised that the partial list of forbidden exports to Italy was having no effect of any importance upon her campaign.   Such sanctions were, like the presence of the British fleet in the Mediterranean, merely serving to exasperate the Italian Government without aiding the Ethiopians.   It was also becoming more and more apparent that far from the Negus being a modern David whose sling and stones could fell the well armed giant, the well-armed giant was doing what efficient and strongly equipped people always do to inefficient and ill-equipped adversaries.

At this time Great Britain chose to give yet another display of half-heartedness and indecision. Italy in Abyssinia was using a mechanised army. Such armies consume great quantities of petrol. Those who were intent upon forcing Italy to abandon her punitive action against the Ethiopians knew well that there might be some effectiveness in adding to the list of exports prohibited by the sanctions-applying nations the oil which the mechanised army and its air force needed for operations.

The Foreign Secretary told the House of Commons that a League Committee was working on oil sanctions and that Britain would take her share in any collective action that might be decided upon. This Committee should have met on November 29th, but at the request of France its meeting was postponed.   This postponement, Sir Samuel Hoare insisted, did not imply any dissension between or weakening of the attitude of the sanction States.

So far Italy had paid little attention to the

League's sanctions, except to protest against their unfairness. Oil sanctions might be a very different matter. There was no question that the Governments of both France and Britain were worried about what might follow if they were rushed into such sanctions by the eighteen committeemen of Geneva. The Foreign Secretary, Sir Samuel Hoare, was frankly eager to bring the conflict to an end before the Eden policy led to a dramatic widening of the scope of Italy's war. There was in his mind the ever-present danger to the ships in the Mediterranean and Britain's known unreadiness for war of any kind. So great was his growing anxiety that a Foreign Office expert, Mr. Petersen, was sent to Paris, there to try to achieve what the League and its various Committees had failed to achieve—the hammering out, with the French Foreign Office, of proposals acceptable both to Italy and Abyssinia. Mr. Petersen and his French interlocutors spent a fortnight in exploring the possibilities, and on December 6th Sir Samuel Hoare, a sick man, broke a holiday journey to Switzerland to take up the conversations.

His visit to Paris gave rise to the famous—or infamous—Hoare-Laval incident. If Britain is to shape her future policy in the light of past errors that incident should be studied with care.

On December 5th the Foreign Secretary, with something of the manner of a fashionable *accoucheur*, assured the Commons that he was "glad to be able to tell the House that the League machinery is working well, and that the Member States for the most part are playing their part." On December 6th, the next day, he arrived in Paris to discuss with M. Laval a peace plan for Abyssinia, and this effort was to be made over the heads of those Member States of which he had spoken, who were, for the most part, finding that the League machinery, far from working well, was having not the slightest effect on Italy's military progress.

Three days were spent with M. Laval. The progress and results of the three days' talk was to have been a profound secret, but there is nothing either secret or sacred in French journalism. The very day that the English visitor left the capital the terms were being discussed freely in the newspapers of Paris.

M. Laval and Sir Samuel Hoare, in their humane anxiety to prevent any further slaughter of the Abyssinians and their desire to pacify Italy and thus prevent a possible world conflict, were prepared to suggest to the Negus of Abyssinia that great tracts of Northern and Southern Ethiopia should be transferred to Italian rule, and a virtual economic control be given to Italy in the Western areas.

We know now that those terms would have been acceptable to Italy and would not have been resisted by the Negus, to whom it was obvious that defeat was inevitable unless Abyssinia was reinforced. It was also obvious to him that the continuance of the war necessitated the fuller arming of the jealous and always menacing Rases (that is, chiefs), so that even had a victory been possible it would be a victory leaving the Emperor with a very precarious foothold in his own domains.

Had these proposals from the Hoare-Laval meeting been allowed to go forward, many thousands of lives would have been saved, the strained but not yet broken friendship of Italy for Britain could have been repaired, the Paris-London-Rome axis could have been preserved and the Rome-Berlin-Tokio axis could not have come into existence.

The proposals were not allowed to go forward. As soon as the terms were unofficially known in Great Britain three things happened. The Leftist Press beat up a gale of sentimental protest which inspired thousands of electors to send postcards and messages to their Members of Parliament. Mr. Anthony Eden, who did not relish his work as the Paladin of the League being superseded by the work of Sir Samuel Hoare as a private negotiator, threatened to resign. Mr. Baldwin lost his nerve.

Mr. Baldwin as Prime Minister had been privy to and had encouraged the visit of Sir Samuel Hoare to M. Laval. A Cabinet meeting held on December 9th after a long discussion—and in the face of Mr. Eden's fury and distress—agreed to sponsor the Hoare-Laval proposals. But in the face of the Press campaign both the proposals and their framer, the Foreign Secretary, had to go. Mr. Eden could not be allowed to resign, for he was the idol of the Peace Balloters and the postcard-sending sentimentalists. Mr. Baldwin decided to throw his colleague, the Foreign Secretary, to the wolves.

In a speech to the Commons he came as near as he could to a confession that the League had disappointed all hopes. One degree nearer to complete frankness would have been tantamount to an abandonment of Geneva. The League, said Mr. Baldwin, was a very human fallible body. The difficulties of keeping it to a continuous policy were almost insuperable. He had always for his own part recognised the possibility of its failing in its earlier efforts to secure peace by collective security.

It might be asked why, if the Premier had so little faith in the League, Britain was placed at hazard by an adherence to it. The answer is that political tactics demanded that adherence for several reasons. Mr. Eden, secure in the thought of the Peace Ballot, the Archbishop's blessing and the heresy hunt which had been raised in the Left-Wing Press, was making resignation a whip with which to compel his leader to abide by the Eden policy. A split in the British Cabinet so soon after the Royal Jubilee and the General Election would have had the worst possible effect on Britain's already damaged standing with the outer world, and Mr. Baldwin knew it. Mr. Eden knew that Mr. Baldwin knew it.

The Prime Minister had approved the Hoare visit, he and his colleagues had approved the fruits of that visit—but Mr. Eden was able to return to Geneva on December 12th and there assure the Committee of Eighteen that the proposals framed by Sir Samuel Hoare and M. Laval were neither "definitive nor sacrosanct." If the League did not approve them, the British representative would have no complaint.

This assurance was given the day before the official text of the Hoare-Laval proposals was made public. With that publicity came another and greater storm of protest from the Left-Wing Press and such bodies as the League of Nations Union, which sent a deputation, headed by Lord Cecil, to admonish the Prime Minister by word of mouth. What the Prime Minister thought as he listened to that deputation we shall never know. He probably did not tell its members that the Foreign Office had already, presumably with his connivance, instructed the British Minister at Addis Ababa, the Ethiopian capital, to use his "utmost influence" to persuade the Emperor to give his careful and favourable consideration to the proposed terms of peace.

Poor Sir Samuel Hoare, still trying to restore his shattered health in Switzerland, had to return home to face a Parliamentary debate. As far as he, or any wise person, knew he had merely discovered, in conjunction with M. Laval, a method of saving thousands of Ethiopians from death and destruction in a hopeless struggle and of snatching back the unarmed British Commonwealth from the brink of a war with the two Totalitarian countries, Italy and Germany. He returned to England on December 16th. On December 18th he resigned.

About that resignation there was something very odd. Here was a Minister who had the full confidence of his leader before, during and after the Paris talks.

In the House of Commons, twelve days before, that leader had said that had his lips been unsealed he could have dissuaded any Member from going into the Division Lobby against him. But here was the leader permitting the Minister to resign as if he were some solitary delinquent! If anybody resigned, surely the leader was the man.

What—the whole country speculated—what could Mr. Baldwin have said had his lips been unsealed? He could certainly have confessed that Britain was in no position to provoke and sustain a war with Italy. He could have said that not Britain and not any one of the League States was ready or able to send armed forces to aid the perishing Abyssinians. He could have said, perhaps, that the French, who had never been eager to put pressure on Italy, were not prepared to march if oil sanctions caused a world war. He said none of these things. It was easier to unseat a colleague than to unseal those strangely closed lips. It was not Sir Samuel Hoare but Mr. Eden who was the pet of the Left-Wing sentimentalists who packed the Albert Hall to cheer politically ignorant clerics, who flooded their favourite organs of opinion with alternate appeals for no armament and war against the Dictators. Mr. Baldwin, if we are to judge him by his own remarks and by the action of the Foreign Office in pressing the Hoare-Laval plan on Ethiopia, knew the right thing at that time was to try to save what was left of Abyssinia and to repair as far as possible the damage done to European amity by the futile policy of sanctions. He preferred to jettison the colleague whose services he had employed, and approved, to bringing this about. This he did to conciliate in advance those critics who in the debate of December 19th might be expected to open fire on his administration. History will not deal tenderly with so flagrant a piece of cowardice in the face of so urgent a need for courage.

Abandoned by a leader whose wish and behest he had too successfully served, Sir Samuel Hoare gave an explanation of his actions which was lucid, manly and unrepentant. Ever since his appointment to the Secretaryship of State for Foreign Affairs he had been obsessed (he said) by two responsibilities. He had to prevent a European war; he had to prevent an isolated war between Britain and Italy. The double duty of the British Government was to take its rightful share in whatever collective action was agreed upon at Geneva and to try to the best of its endeavours to find a basis of settlement acceptable to both parties to the Abyssinian dispute. He considered that a turning point had been reached about a fortnight before the day on which he spoke. The prohibition of the export of oil to Italy was being considered, and oil sanctions—it was known— would be regarded by Italy not as an extension of economic sanctions but as the imposition of a military sanction. Oil Sanctions would mean war with Italy. The danger was immediate and the attack might be launched on Britain before she had the support of other Powers. His task had been, he considered, to

MR. NEVILLE CHAMBERLAIN

do something which would obviate the necessity for
an oil embargo, and to this end the energies of
himself and M. Laval had been directed. His own
task, he frankly said, had not been any easier by
reason of the need to preserve the solidarity of the
Anglo-French relationship, which, he confessed, had
not been too securely based. This had meant that
the British Foreign Secretary had had to make some
concessions to the French.

In making this speech Sir Samuel Hoare recognised
that the proposals were now dead and uttered the
grave warning that, as a result, the situation was now
far more acute than it had been. The only alternative he saw to the jettisoned proposals was the full
co-operation in the military sphere, if necessary, of all
the League States. In the event this proved not to
be the alternative. Abyssinia was permitted to fight
on without either oil sanctions or military aid in
the diminishing expectation of practical help until
she reached utter defeat.

This episode in our foreign policy had far-reaching
effects. Under Mr. Eden's lead, Britain and the
other League States had shown to the world that
they were completely ineffective when faced by a
determined Power. This was an enormous stimulus
to the militarists of Japan and Germany. It caused
the small nations which had hitherto looked upon
Britain as a kind of strong defender to lose faith in
British sincerity and strength, and to turn towards
the Totalitarian States.

When on December 23rd, 1935, it was announced

8

that Mr. Eden had become Foreign Secretary in Sir
Samuel Hoare's place the implication was obvious—
Britain had ceased to have a foreign policy other
than that dictated by the resolutions of the medley
of nations at Geneva, where Russia and France
wielded the dominant influence. This alignment
meant that Britain automatically became suspect by
the anti-Red Powers.

As Mr. Winston Churchill said, on April 6th, 1936:
"We have managed to secure all the disadvantages
without any of the advantages. We have pressed
France into a course of action which did not go far
enough to help Ethiopia, but went far enough to
sever us from Italy, with the result that the occasion
was given to Hitler to tear up the Treaty and re-
occupy the Rhineland." We had also gone far
enough to assure Japan that as Italy had flouted
Britain and the League in the West, the Japanese
might flout them in the East.

On the very day that Mr. Churchill spoke, Mr. Eden
belatedly told the Commons that several lessons were
to be learned from the dispute. These included
the lessons that:

> The League, limited in Membership, is inevitably limited
> in effectiveness.
>
> Financial and economic sanctions cannot be immediately
> effective if Membership of the League is not complete.

These to a normal mind were not lessons to be
learned but self-evident truths. Mr. Eden's course
of instruction had been costly for Britain—costly in
money, in trade and in prestige.

He further confessed himself as not being confident that British action in this instance would be effective in combatting aggression, but he hoped it would be an inspiring example for the future.

This remarkable statement was tantamount to saying that although your attempt to-day to knock down a brick wall by running your head against it may be a disastrous failure, it should inspire you to try again on some other brick wall some other day.

British Foreign policy at this time was more than usually baffling to foreigners and embarrassing to patriotic Britons who cared for the standing of their country. There was, for example, another curious example of Mr. Eden's divided mind. In February he told the House of Commons that oil sanctions must wait until it could be shown that they would be effective and then earned a rebuke from M. Flandin for saying at Geneva that Britain was in favour of oil sanctions.

Mr. Baldwin, to check growing anxiety about the possible effect of what the Press called Mr. Eden's strong words at Geneva, told his own constituents that he wished "to make it clear beyond all doubt that the policy the Foreign Secretary is conducting in this matter is not his own personal policy but the considered policy of the whole Government."

But what was the policy?

Mr. Eden wanted stronger pressure of sanctions against Italy but could not support France in a desire to apply sanctions against Germany if that nation fortified the Rhine.

Sanctions had proved totally unable to stay Italy's victorious campaign in Abyssinia but had been so fraught with the danger of precipitating a European war that Britain from the first had had to keep a fleet in the Mediterranean, trusting to France to provide ports if the vessels were attacked—and yet Mr. Eden could say at Geneva, on April 20th, that Britain considered the League, which he had already called ineffective because of its limited membership, as "the best instrument at present available for the preservation of international peace."

What was to be made of these differing and contradictory attitudes?

On May 6th Mr. Eden said in the Commons that:

> . . . throughout this dispute and the negotiations since the war broke out we ourselves have taken the lead. That may or may not have been right. There may be two views about it. . .

There were two views. One was shared between those who months before had forecast what must be the ignominious result of his policy and the wretched Negus of Abyssinia who having taken seriously the brave words at Geneva was now in exile, his land lost and thousands of his subjects slain.

Mr. Eden said frankly, "We have to face the fact that we have got to admit the failure of the League," and added that "it is clear the League must go on."

For some reason, although the war was over, sanctions, too, had to "go on." The small nations, like Yugoslavia and Greece, had good practical reasons for desiring their continuance. With sanctions went a pledge of mutual assistance against Italy. But Britons were actually being injured by sanctions. They had no reason for wishing them to continue. They could not help Abyssinia, for Abyssinia was already betrayed and defeated.

Even Mr. Eden at last realised how preposterous and dangerous it was to subject Italy to sanctions now the war was over. In the June of 1936 he took the lead in dropping them, admitting that they had failed, but blaming the experts who had misled him and his Geneva colleagues as to the duration of the war. On the 23rd of that month the House of Commons held a kind of memorial service over the dead policy. Nobody was very happy. The leader of the Opposition—for whose support the Government had sacrificed so much, including honour and Sir Samuel Hoare—said, truthfully if unkindly:

> Mr. Eden stood very high in the opinion of the men and women of this country: he has forfeited that. He has had the difficult choice between two loyalties. He seems to have said, "What does it profit a man if he gains the whole world, and lose the old school tie."

Mr. Baldwin, who, when the National Government was formed, so readily parted with Sir Austen Chamberlain on the score of age, now tried to excuse Mr. Eden on the grounds of youth. "I am much older than he. I know the disappointment to him has been keen. He started with higher hopes of what was possible than I did."

The mischief was done. As Mr. Cocks told the

House of Commons, "Abyssinia has been conquered, the League has been destroyed, British prestige and honour are lying in the dust," a sentence that led its utterer to perhaps the aptest quotation that has ever been used in a Parliamentary debate—"I conclude with a few words used by a great statesman, Benjamin Disraeli, Earl of Beaconsfield, on July 4th, 1864: 'We will not threaten and then refuse to act. We will not lure on our Allies with expectations we do not expect to fulfil. And, Sir, if ever we have the honour to act, to carry on important negotiations on behalf of this country, I trust that we at least shall not carry them on in such a manner that it will be our duty to come to Parliament to announce to the country that we have no allies and then declare that England can never act alone . . . ' "

The real and final commentary on Mr. Eden's policy of sanction-mongering came not, however, from that long dead voice. It came from Mr. Eden, who said on September 21st, 1937, about Japan, what he should have said on October 5th, 1935, about Italy:

> If Hon. Members are advocating sanctions by the League, if they think the League ought to impose sanctions in the present dispute . . . I would remind them that there are two possible forms of sanctions—the ineffective which are not worth putting on, and the effective which means the risk, if not the certainty, of war. I say deliberately that nobody would contemplate any action of that kind unless they are convinced that they have overwhelming force to back their policy.
>
> Do Rt. Hon. gentlemen opposite really think that the

League of Nations to-day, with only two great naval Powers in it, ourselves and France, have got that overwhelming force ? It must be clear to everyone that that overwhelming force does not exist.

The whole fiasco of the attempt of Britain through Geneva to impose her will upon Italy was due, it will have been seen, precisely to the fault which Mr. Eden in those words attributed to the "Rt. Hon. gentlemen" opposite. Neither he nor his colleagues under Mr. Baldwin's leadership had foreseen that lacking overwhelming force and a readiness to use it the League could only be derided by a nation supplied with such force and quite ready to use it. He had fallen into the error, long before rebuked by von Clausewitz, that there was some "benevolent" means, such as sanctions, of imposing the will of the League upon Italy. He had been active in putting on ineffective sanctions which were not worth putting on, well knowing that in Britain's unarmed state the effective sanctions which would almost certainly have meant war could not be put on. In consequence, Britain was made to look like a blustering but futile poacher-turned-gamekeeper.

CHAPTER VIII

THE EMERGENCE OF HITLER

"That young man believes what he says; he will go far."

MIRABEAU, *of Robespierre.*

THE wild swirl of emotion which filled the British people when Italy moved against Abyssinia is understandable. Had it been an emotion rising from a knowledge of facts, it would have been commendable. The common impression that the Abyssinians were a simple, guileless pastoral people set upon by land-hungry aggressors from merely predatory motives was exactly that which would stir all the traditional sympathy of Britons for the under dog. There was no endeavour made to instruct the British masses in Italy's side of the case. Even when Marconi himself, the inventor to whom broadcasting owed its possibility, desired to speak on the radio to a British audience in exposition of Italy's view, permission was denied to him, an act of discourtesy which no bitterness of political feeling can excuse.

For a year or more before the outbreak of the Abyssinian war those publicists who had tried to impress on the British public that British armament wa s in desperate need of repair had been derided as alar mists or denounced as mere war-mongers. When th at war began the statesmen responsible for Britain's we akness in arms were not prepared to confess that they were now unable to exert sufficient force in international affairs to insist upon the conflict being either abandoned or postponed.

This inability arose from a complete misjudgment of what had happened to Germany with the advent there to power of Herr Hitler. For this misjudgment Mr. Anthony Eden must bear the major blame. From 1926, when he was appointed Parliamentary Private Secretary to Sir Austen Chamberlain, the then Foreign Secretary, Mr. Eden, had unique opportunities for mastering the complexities of those international relations and affairs with which he was later to deal as the youngest Foreign Secretary since Lord Greville took office in 1791. To him was given a close and intimate acquaintance with the changing personalities who thronged the European scene, and the new forces that were sweeping it.

Despite this terrific advantage, Mr. Eden failed entirely to grip the significance of two historic moments in European history. The first was when, on March 16th, 1935, Herr Hitler, without warning, decreed the re-introduction of conscription in Germany. The second was when, some ten days later, he told the British Foreign Secretary, in Berlin, that Germany had reached parity with Great Britain in the air. The second of these moments had a significance that no statesman should have missed, for the German Leader told Sir John Simon that Germany took no interest in collective security, although, on her own terms, she might consider rejoining the League of Nations. Had Mr. Eden really grasped the significance of Germany's new position and recovered military strength he would never, surely, at that very time, have concerted a diplomatic mission to Moscow into a kind of love-feast with Germany's inveterate enemy, M. Litvinof, the ertswhile Mr. Finklestein.

To a Minister of State, charged with the safety of a whole nation, there is not permitted that free indulgence in personal emotions and antipathies which a private citizen can enjoy without responsibility. The private citizen may look at the nations about him and hate one and love the other. He may retch at the bloodstained record of Bolshevist Russia, or be nauseated by the grim methods of Fascism and Nazism. A statesman charged with the well-being of his fellow-countrymen may, indeed, feel such emotions, but he cannot allow himself to be governed by them. His policy must be governed by facts as they are, not as he thinks they ought to be. He cannot afford to denounce such nations as may answer his denunciation by attack from the air upon the defenceless ports through which his countrymen are fed. He cannot link himself to one political philosophy if that means that his nation is made thereby the immediate object of antagonism to other nations to whom that philosophy is anathema.

The very basis of the League of Nations was the admission by all its Members that no nation had any right to interfere with the internal affairs of other nations. Russia might hate the capitalist system of Britain, but she had no right to endeavour to change it. Britain might dislike the system adopted by Italy, but she had no right to endeavour by pressure to have it altered.   It would be folly to deny that in Britain there was a very wide and deep-seated antagonism to both Fascism and Nazism, just as there was a similar hatred of Bolshevism.   Mr. Baldwin realised this when he said: "I know perfectly well how many feel about the Nazi regime.   I know that there are many who regard with some disfavour a regime which lies farther East.   But let us look for a moment at what is the cause of this regime in Germany, and let us, in passing, draw a lesson from it ourselves.   Germany lost the War, she paid a great price in the peace treaties, and she was left with very inconsiderable armaments, and we all hoped that disarmament was coming in Europe.   I need not here go into the various reasons that made those conferences fail and how the countries of Europe lagged, but we do know that during those unhappy years which that country went through after the War she was very near to a state of revolution.   The German is naturally a law-abiding man, and he had a glimpse into the abyss when Communism in Germany raised its head—and Communism was a creed of violence and force.   It was beaten ultimately by another creed of violence and force, and you have that great people who during many years have seen the regime that *would* and the regime that *did* found itself on force, and what wonder that the idea of force—not an alien idea to the Teuton—should seem to dominate very much that mentality to-day."

In that passage Mr. Baldwin, for once, placed a finger on the central fact concerning the Nazi regime in Germany. In a phrase borrowed from an earlier Prime Minister, Mr. Baldwin also assured his hearers on another occasion that Britain's frontiers are on the Rhine. It was a variation of the old adage that Britain's frontiers are the coast lines of the enemy, for in our days of aerial warfare the words "coast lines" must be construed metaphorically. By all the instincts of self-preservation and all the dictates of commonsense, it behoves a nation to be friendly with a strong neighbour over a dangerous boundary line, until and unless that neighbour actively threatens aggression. There was, when Herr Hitler came into power in Germany, every reason why Britain and Germany should be friendly.

The Nazi regime, like the Fascist regime in Italy' had as its *raison d'être* the preservation of the land from the Leftism which had made first a slaughter-house and next a poorhouse of Russia. Both Hitler and Mussolini owed their political being to their antagonism to Bolshevism, that very Bolshevism which had from the first avowed its intention to end "the capitalist British Empire." Far from Nazism and Fascism being in their origin antagonistic to British interests, they were the bulwarks of those interests.

By a right understanding of Hitler, Britain could have ensured the peace of the world for generations to come and would have avoided the armaments race which is now crippling all nations alike.

Let us look at the history and position of Germany in 1934 as any European statesman, Mr. Eden for example, must have known it to be, remembering always that in dealing with men and nations it is necessary not only to know the facts, but how those facts are interpreted by all whom they affect.

In the war of 1914-18 the German people entered the conflict convinced that they were fighting for their very existence against a "ring of steel" which the machinations of foreign diplomacy had welded about them. In such a belief they may have been misled by evil counsellors, but they were sincere enough. They fought with a dogged and superb courage. None who fought against them will question their devotion and their heroism. They were defeated largely by a naval blockade which starved the women and children behind the lines as effectively as it put their troops on short rations in the field. This blockade was effected by a British Minister of Blockade, then Lord Robert Cecil, now Lord Cecil of Chelwood. The end of the war was not a collapse of the German military front but of the German home front. In saying this one does not belittle in any way the marvellous war effort in the field of the Allied troops or on the seas of the Fleets, nor does one underrate the effect of the fresh American divisions which were ready to pour into the line in 1918. Soldiers and sailors won the war, but it would not have ended when it did, or even how it did, but for the blockade aided by the pressure of Allied war propaganda operating on the blockade-starved civilian population.

In March, 1918, the Germans were within an ace of winning.   The Allies had "their backs to the wall." By the early Autumn the tide had turned.   The German people were being told through all sources of Allied propaganda that it was not they but their military caste, the Junkers, whom the Allies were fighting.   They were being told that the Allied peoples were not fighting for territorial aggrandisement, but to make the world safe for democracy.

President Wilson, that great American idealist, in what became known as the "Four Point Speech" and in a Note containing the famous Fourteen Points, was drawing the German nation towards peace.   In the September of 1918, after the failure of the big German offensive on the Western Front, the Foreign Secretary, von Hintze (who was at General Headquarters) prepared for his Foreign Office this message:

> On the strength of His Majesty's command and with the agreement of the Imperial Chancellor at Vienna, kindly inform Constantinople confidentially that I propose to suggest peace to President Wilson on the basis of his fourteen points, and to invite him to call a peace conference at Washington, at the same time asking for an immediate cessation of hostilities.*

It was not, however, until October 3rd that the message was sent.   In a reply received on October 8th the United States Secretary of State, Mr. Robert

*"Preliminary History of the Armistice." Carnegie Endowment for International Peace. 1924.

Lancing, asked, among other questions, whether the Germans accepted in full the conditions of peace laid down by President Wilson in his speech of January 8th and subsequent addresses.   On October 14th the German Government replied that it accepted the principles which the President had laid down in the January and other speeches.   In an exchange of Notes which followed Mr. Lancing virtually asked for the expulsion of the German Emperor.   His Note remarked that it was evident that the German people had no means of commanding the acquiescence of the military authorities and that the "power of the King of Prussia to control the policy of the Empire is unimpaired."   If the Government of the United States, said the Note, "must deal with the military masters and the monarchical autocrats of Germany now, or if it is likely to have to deal with them later in regard to the international obligations of the German Empire, it must demand, not peace negotiations, but surrender."

Cessation of hostilities thus depended upon two conditions to be observed by Germany—the abandonment of the Kaiser and his military autocracy and the acceptance of President Wilson's peace points.

If the people of Britain are to understand Nazi Germany, and if British policy towards Germany is to be soundly based, it is essential that these peace points be themselves first understood.   They are to be found, chiefly, in two speeches, that of January 8th, 1918, containing the Fourteen Points, and that of February 11th containing the Four Points.   The

simplest way of verifying my version of them is by
reference to the "Encyclopædia Britannica," 14th
edition, 1929, on pages 565 and 566.

Of the Fourteen Points three are especially interesting. They are:

> (3) The removal, as far as possible, of all economic
> barriers and the establishment of an equality of trade
> conditions among all nations consenting to the peace and
> associating themselves for its maintenance.
>
> (4) Adequate guarantees given and taken that national
> armaments will be reduced to the lowest point consistent
> with domestic safety.
>
> (5) A free, open-minded, and absolutely impartial adjust-
> ment of all colonial claims, based upon a strict observance
> of the principle that in determining all such questions of
> sovereignty the interests of the populations concerned
> must have equal weight with the equitable claims of the
> Government whose title is to be determined.

The speech of February 11th contained re-
affirmations of these principles. The second and third
of the points were:

> . . . Peoples and provinces are not to be bartered about
> from sovereignty to sovereignty as if they were chattels or
> pawns in a game, even the great game, now for ever dis-
> credited, of the balance of power, but that
>
> Every territorial settlement involved in this war must be
> made in the interest and for the benefit of the populations
> concerned, and not as part of any mere adjustment or com-
> promise of claims amongst rival States.

These points and principles were still further
elaborated by the American President in further
speeches, the "Four Ends" speech of July 4th and
the "Five Particulars" speech of September 27th,

SIGNOR MUSSOLINI AND HERR HITLER

but the speech of February 11th was the most vital. In it President Wilson declared without equivocation or mental reservation whatsoever that:

THERE SHALL BE NO ANNEXATIONS, NO CONTRIBUTIONS, NO PUNITIVE DAMAGES.

Germany was commanded to accept these principles. There is no question that the other Allies accepted them, for during an exchange of Notes in the period May-June, 1919, between them and Germany, they affirmed that they were in complete accord with the German delegation that the basis for the negotiation of the Treaty was to be found in the correspondence immediately preceding the Armistice.

It was there agreed that the Treaty of Peace should be based upon the Fourteen Points of President Wilson's address of January 8th, 1918 . . . and upon the principles of settlement enunciated by President Wilson in his later addresses, and particularly in his address of September 27th, 1918. These are the principles upon which hostilities were abandoned. . .

"The principles upon which hostilities were abandoned" have been well analysed and set out by Mr. de Montgomery in his study "Versailles" and are as follows:

(1) Germany surrendered on the express condition that the peace terms would not be dictated to her, but would conform to those previously agreed upon.

(2) By the fulfilment of the conditions of the Armistice Germany not only furnished proof of her unequivocal acceptance of the terms of the pre-Armistice agreement, but created an obligation

9

on the part of the Allies to fulfil their share of the contract.

(3) Both the German and the Allied Governments have recognised the fact that a "pactum de contrahendo" had been concluded between them previous to the Armistice, and that the peace should be based upon the conditions of that agreement.

(4) In the absence of any judicial body to settle disputes out of the interpretation of the general terms of peace agreed upon before the Armistice, the Allied governments were in a position to enforce their own opinion in all matters of interpretation— yet Germany has still the right to a revision of the Treaty where an obvious misinterpretation or violation of the terms of the pre-Armistice agreement has taken place.

(5) The pre-Armistice agreement is legally binding on the Allies even if it should be proved that the German Army was actually beaten in the field at the moment of signing the Armistice. High military authorities of both sides have, however, given evidence that the German army was still in a position to inflict heavy losses on the enemy right up to the moment of the Armistice, and that the Allies gained great advantages and avoided much sacrifice by Germany's surrender.

(6) The following terms form part of the pre-Armistice agreement:

(a) The Allies do not wish to injure Germany or to block in any way her legitimate influence or power.

(*b*) Germany to live on equal terms of liberty and safety with the Allies.

(*c*) Adequate guarantees given and taken that the national armaments will be reduced to the lowest point consistent with domestic safety.

(*d*) As there is to be equality as regards safety, France is under the obligation to reduce her armaments to the same level as Germany.

(*e*) Absolutely impartial adjustment of all colonial claims.

(*f*) No annexations, either of European or colonial territory.

(*g*) No contributions, no punitive damages—Germany, however, to make compensation for damage done to the civilian population of the Allies and their property.

The Wilsonian principles also involved recognition of the fact that the war had its roots in the disregard of the rights of small nations, and that special alliances and economic rivalries have been the prolific source in the modern world of plans that produce war.

We reach now that which to German eyes seems the great betrayal, and to British eyes unblinded by prejudice can seem little different.

On the strength of the pre-Armistice agreement Germany did two things.

She exiled the Kaiser and abandoned the military caste.

She agreed to the Wilsonian points as a basis for armistice.

What was the result?

Peace was dictated to her and not negotiated.

She was disarmed but European armament increased.

She was stripped of her colonies and territory
was annexed by the Allies.

Economic barriers were not removed and no
attempt was made to achieve equality of
trade among the post-war States.

If it is held that Germany was the blood-guilty
nation and that she was thoroughly defeated in the
War she invoked, then it is natural to hold, also, that
whatever was done to her was deserved.   If Germany
was blood-guilty, then the Germans "got what was
coming to them."   But if that view is held, there
should never have been any pre-Armistice agreement.
The word of the Allies—Great Britain's word—should
never have been pledged.   Whether Germany was
blood-guilty or not, the word *was* pledged, and *was*
broken.

Germany herself never accepted, and does not now
accept, the view that she was blood-guilty, nor the
view that she was thoroughly defeated in the field.
Nine days before the Armistice one of the German
High-Command told his Government that "the
German army is still strong enough to stand against
its opponents for months to come, to achieve local
success and exact new sacrifices from the enemy."

We are not here concerned to argue the rightness of
either viewpoint.   We are concerned only to note the
indisputable fact that, whatever the guilt of Germany
in 1914 and whatever the state of her armies in 1918,
she accepted an armistice on terms that were afterwards deliberately broken.

The "Treaty" was handed to her, metaphorically,

on the point of a bayonet. It was, therefore, not a treaty at all, since the very word means an agreement reached by negotiation. The German Empire was stripped of its overseas possessions. These were the two most glaring breaches of faith which rankled in the bosoms of the German people long after the War had ended. That Germany should be disarmed while her small and vindictive neighbours were strongly arming rankled only less bitterly.

What followed?

The events in post-war Germany have been often described. To avoid any suspicion of over-statement arising from personal prejudice I extract a striking account from a "book written from the standpoint of observers who would place their faith in the old democracy rather than in new dictatorship," which was published in 1935. It is "The Way of the Dictators," by Lewis Broad and Leonard Russell.

With admirable restraint they write:

> The economic distress in Germany in the decade following the War was more severe than anything known in England in modern times. It fell short, certainly, of the famine in Russia, but the German people endured privations unparalleled among civilised races in our day. As a result of the Allied blockade—*which continued for some months after the War ended*—there was a scarcity of all kinds of food. The nation lost much of its power of resistence to illness and infection; ill-nourishment produced a mental inertia in adults; children were to be seen suffering from hunger madness.
>
> These were the conditions that saw the birth of Hitlerism.
>
> The blockade was lifted; the standard of living gradually improved, but it remained, and remains, below the level in

England and France. The working classes had a grim struggle for existence. There was the nightmare for the nation of the catastrophic plunges of the Mark, when as paper money was churned out by the printing presses the people's wealth and savings vanished. There was a respite, and then Germany felt the onset of the world economic blizzard. The chaos of national bankruptcy again appeared imminent. Trade and industry collapsed, men went out of work thousand after thousand, until at one time it was estimated that the unemployed touched a figure of ten millions.

This is the background, these are the conditions, which explain the rise of Hitlerism. The older democratic parties appeared to be failing in the maintenance of the old order. The people turned to Hitler as a strong man who could save the country from Bolshevism. The older parties were conscious of the limitations of their ability and power. Hitler was conscious of the national aspirations, and proclaimed his ability to bring about their fulfilment.

As Messrs. Broad and Russell, and every knowledgeable commentator on modern Germany, agree and emphasise, there was an even more galling punishment for the Germans than material hardship. The nation had suffered the humiliation of defeat in war; it had suffered the humiliation of being held to be the guilty party for the loss of the millions who had died in the conflict. In the years following the defeat those who had suffered and endured, but had had the ill-luck not to be killed, were treated as malefactors. They were not regarded as national heroes, but as national objects of abuse and contempt. They were invited to feel not pride for their ardours and endurances, but shame and penitence.

Their nation as a whole was humiliated, but they were doubly humiliated. Such suffering, humiliation, and despair was the cradle of Hitlerism.

But whatever circumstances cradled Hitlerism, it would not have come to birth without Hitler.

The failure of the British statesmen and public to understand Hitler and Hitlerism in their earliest days has been responsible for the whole drift and error of British foreign policy. The derision with which the acknowledged saviour of Germany was hailed as a kind of political Charlie Chaplin, an imitative buffoon striving to mimic Mussolini, himself still derided, was understandable, though not pardonable, in ignorant electoral masses. It was neither understandable nor pardonable in circles where men were expected to have a close knowledge of contemporary events and forces in Europe.

Herr Hitler, to the eyes of the British Parliamentarians, was a strange figure. No career could have been in greater contrast with that of a typical successful young Parliamentarian, such as, for example, Mr. Eden. These two men were, broadly speaking, of the same generation. The one was the son of an artistic and titled father. He had passed from an ancient public school to a commission in a famous regiment and from thence to a job on the Staff. After the war he had gone to an ancient university and had there taken a brilliant first-class in Oriental languages. Entry to Parliament had been made easy for him, a safe seat following the usual onslaught on a strongly-contested seat. Once in Parliament, family and friendly connections had made a rise to Office almost automatic.   How different was the record of the other!

Hitler's father was a cobbler who rose to the dignity of a petty Customs official.   The youth, after an unsuccessful attempt to become an artist and an architect, was a bricklayer's labourer, poor and often hungry.   As an Austrian he was frankly and ingenuously gratified to be allowed to serve in a Bavarian regiment as a private soldier.   As a battalion runner—most unenviable and dangerous of occupations—he displayed marked heroism and was awarded the Iron Cross.   A little before the armistice he was the victim of a British gas attack near to Ypres, and was in hospital when the War ended.

Between the two men the only qualities in common were a proved personal courage and patriotism.

Different as Herr Hitler was from the familiar type of British politician, anybody who had watched Germany in her recurring ordeals should have grasped the fact at his emergence that he was, like Naopleon before him, not merely a man, but a portent.   His method of coming to power should have told the observers in other countries that he would be a force with which to be reckoned, whether for good or evil.

Two emotions were strong in the youthful Hitler. One was a feeling of revolt against the tyranny of trades unionism, which had once robbed him of his humble means of livelihood.   The other was a repugnance engendered in him by a Jew whom he saw in Vienna.   Added to these after the War must have been an emotion even stronger, an emotion between rage and hatred at the plight of his country and the plight of his fellow soldiers, now under the dregs of men. The scorn of the fighting soldier for the shirking civilian is always deep. It drives to the very soul of a man when the shirking civilian himself turns scornful at the fool who fought and suffered when he might have been comfortably joining in the scramble for personal wealth behind the lines. Germany emerged from the War a defeated nation, but the land-grabbing Jews and the clever profit-snatching gentiles seemed to have made a good thing out of defeat. They were only one degree less odious than the scum which, under the leadership of Left-Wing doctrinaires, was preparing to seize power from the well-meaning but inept Republican political leaders.

In the midsummer of 1919 young Hitler became the seventh member of the inner circle of a small "party" of forty members calling itself the "German Workers' Party." His joining this body was, probably, the most accidental thing of his career, for at the moment of his reception into it he was contemplating the formation of a party of his own. But once a member, he turned his talents for organisation and oratory unsparingly to its use. The little party soon grew.

Shortly after his admission to the party Hitler devised a twenty-five point programme. Of these points the most vital were those which covered the necessity for:

A united community of Germans.

The wiping out of the Peace Treaties.

The return of the colonies.

The abolition of unearned incomes.

The recognition of the Jew as an alien.

To that programme Hitler has remained, and will remain, faithful. It is the key to war and peace in Europe. As such it should long ago have been recognised by all responsible statesmen. Such recognition does not imply agreement with its rightness. Whether right or wrong, justified or unjustified, it is the aim to which Germany steadily works.

When the 25 Point Programme was drawn up Hitler was unknown outside a small circle of discontented Germans. The document was then as wild a piece of romanticism as the wonderful will which was drawn up by the almost moneyless young undergraduate Cecil Rhodes. Even had the leaders of other nations been aware of it, they could have been excused for not taking seriously so grotesque a programme from so insignificant a personage. That was in 1919. Neither the document nor its author should have been misconstrued in the January of 1933, for between those two dates much happened, of which the average British elector is probably still unaware or only hazily informed.

By 1920 the party which had attracted Hitler had grown both in numbers and aggressiveness. It had been re-named the National Socialist German Workers' Party. One of its objects and activities was to prevent, by force if necessary, the holding of meetings or lectures which might poison the minds of German citizens with Marxism. Hitler himself for his personal violence in this cause was sentenced to three months imprisonment, two-thirds of the sentence being remitted.

It is this resort to violence which the British mind, attuned to many years of freedom of speech, finds incomprehensible and repugnant in the history of the Nazi and Fascist movements. Bred in the belief that "force is no remedy," the Briton revolts from political movements which use force as their primary weapon. This is odd, for it was from Britain that Italians and Germans had their early lessons in the application of force to political disputes. It is not, for example, without significance that one of the best biographies of Cromwell is by an Italian. It is still more significant that in the formative years of both Signor Mussolini and Herr Hitler Britain appeared to readers of the foreign news in Italian and German newspapers to be perpetually the scene of political applications of force. Asquith, the great Liberal Prime Minister, had been enjoined as Home Secretary to "remember Featherstone," where workers had been shot down by the military. Balfour, grown into a placid philosopher-statesman, had made his early reputation by coercing the Irish and uttering the famous order, "Do not hesitate to shoot!" Sir Edward Carson had armed and drilled militant Ulstermen. Women had paved the way to the feminine franchise by displays of ragged violence. The North West frontier of India was hardly held by the terrorism of the screw-gun and, later, the aeroplane. And these things were done, and rightly done in view of the social need, by a nation whose tranquillity was not menaced by any really devastating disruptive movement.   Reading of the day-to-day commerce of political life in Britain, the young foreigner who cared to note such things learnt of baton charges against the unemployed, against strikers, and knew that in many supposedly peaceful democratic constituencies candidates could not hold meetings without police protection.   The world-wide publicity given to the lives of the democratic statesmen who had moulded the Treaty of Versailles had taught everybody that even Mr. Lloyd George had once been smuggled away from a roaring and forceful mob disguised as a policeman.   In the democratic United States, the traditional land of freedom, the application of force in the shape of the cop's baton or the soldiery's tear bombs was a commonplace of minority politics.

The violence of the infant Nazi movement was, thus, not a reversion to barbaric type.   It was a regrettable emulation of the political habits of those very democracies which deprecated it.   And, as Mr. Baldwin told the House of Commons, it was violence applied to a movement itself relying largely on violence for its progress.

Actually the use of physical force by the young Hitler movement was auxiliary to the use of educational propaganda.   By the end of 1920 the little body of 40 members had grown to 3,000 and a newspaper had been bought.

All these activities were conducted at Munich, but

Hitler was ready for a larger sphere of action. It was as if a young Ulsterman, of terrific faith in the ultimate destiny of the British race, after serving with distinction in, say, the Lancashire Fusiliers, had begun a patriotic movement in Glasgow amongst the razor-slashing Reds. The natural inclination of such an agitator after the dawn of local success to the movement would be to make his impress on London, the capital city. Hitler was actually in Berlin when, in 1921, an attempt was made by his colleagues to undermine his position with the party of which he was propagandist-in-chief. The result of that attempt was his election to the party Presidency under a new constitution which gave him unlimited powers. Not his enemies but himself had achieved a coup.

This abortive attack on his standing with the infant National Socialist Party had one far-reaching effect. He formed the now famous S.A.—the Brownshirts, the Storm Troopers. These were a picked body of men, a defence corps, who were Hitler's personal instrument, although officially they were declared to be merely a section of the movement "devoted to gymnastics and sport."

The Brownshirts have been freely displayed as a band of Bashi-Basouks organised for sheer brutal terrorism, a sadistic band of young ruffians. Nothing could be further from the truth of their origin. Brutal they proved to be, for they confronted a brutal situation, and revolutions are neither made nor countered in kid gloves. But the significance of this body is to be found in a curious episode wherein Hitler's command of his new guard was threatened.

Germany was inflamed at the provision of the Treaty which forbade her an army while her neighbours were under no such prohibition. A certain Captain Röhm, who had been instrumental in acquiring the newspaper for the movement, desired that the stalwarts of the S.A. should form part of a secret army and that Reichswehr officers should be in command of their training. In the event the storm troops were put under the command of a new recruit to the National Socialist movement, a re-markable man with a remarkable war record who had been converted by Hitler's oratory. His name was Hermann Göring. He had been one of the most redoubtable air aces of the War and an ornament of the Richthofen Circus, which when Richthofen was shot down he commanded. His exploits had been the talk of all armies on the Western front and he had been awarded the highest decoration for valour—the German V.C.—the Order of Merit. He was both brave and efficient, by no means a common con-junction, a large genial comrade but given to outbursts of furious temper. He was a man both loved and feared.

The first dramatic attempt to seize power by the new party was the abortive *putsch* of Munich, the history of which need not again be rehearsed in these pages. Politically it was an abject failure; the marchers to Berlin were scattered. But it demon-strated strikingly the physical courage and the spiritual determination of Hitler, Göring and their companions. Göring was hit, but Hitler escaped with a damaged shoulder, sustained while taking cover to escape a fusillade from the infantry against which the procession persisted in marching.

The planners of the march had to face the courts and a possible death penalty. Hitler took the occasion to address his judges with great fire. "It was not he who was on trial," says one commentator, "it was the Government."

His harangue from the dock caused his sentence to be much lighter than might have been expected. He was condemned to five years detention in a fortress with the proviso that, if his conduct merited it, he could be released earlier. He stayed pent in his prison for some months, during which he occupied his time in the writing of an autobiography, the testament known as *Mein Kampf*, of which Britain still awaits a full translation.

The abortive *putsch* did much for Hitler. It made the National Socialist movement illegal, and detached his Storm Troops from the Reichswehr. This enabled Hitler, on his release, to re-organise his party on a new basis of complete personal autocracy. In Berlin Dr. Goebbels took charge of propaganda. As with Talleyrand, a physical disability turned him from the more active services and, like Talleyrand again, he disclosed a mastery of political strategy which made him the true complement of the two executive officers of the party in Munich. The organisation became fully national. The original

40 members grew to 40,000 in 1927, to 120,000 in
1929 and to 250,000 in 1930.

In that year the Party gained 107 seats in the
Reichstag. It was the second largest party in that
assembly, some 6,500,000 votes having been cast for
Hitler, whose accession to complete power was now
becoming only a matter of time.

Circumstances were in full tide behind him.
Germany was again on the very verge of bankruptcy.
Salaries and wages were suffering great and savage
cuts. The Treasury was empty. Reparation payments under the Young Plan were making more than
ever unpopular the Peace Treaty for the repudiation
of which Hitler stood. Dr. Brüning, the Chancellor,
was having to take refuge in decrees, for the democratic machine was failing in its functions.

About this time the Foreign Ministers of other
nations had an unexpected demonstration of how
strongly behind the new Nazi movement the German
populace was gathering. The first presidential term
of the aged and adulated Hindenburg was ending.
Hitler offered himself as a candidate. On the first
poll he received 11,000,000 votes against the old
Field Marshal's 18,500,000. On the second poll he
had 13,000,000 against Hindenburg's 19,000,000.

Bruning gave way to von Papen as Chancellor, von
Papen to von Schleicher.

Von Schleicher was unable to control the animosity
of the Junkers.

On January 31st, 1933, Hitler, the ex-Corporal,
became Chancellor of the Reich.

Chapter IX

BRITAIN DEGRADED

Are there any further degradations waiting for us?
MR. GALLACHER, M.P., *in the Commons to Mr. Eden.*

FOR those foreign observers who underrated the power and significance of Herr Hitler when he became Chancellor there is one thing to be said. He seemed to be in office only by the goodwill of his opponents. He was running in triple harness with von Papen and Hugenberg. His position was very much that of Napoleon at the time of the Consulate. Not until the election of March 5th 1933, would it be possible for Europe rightly to assess the weight of the new German Chancellor.

Before that polling date, however, came the burning of the Reichstag, which changed the whole complexion of German affairs. The cause of that fire will provide historians with a first-class dispute for generations to come. Whatever its origin— Communist or other—Hitler well knew its import. To von Papen he said, at the scene of the fire, "This is a God-given signal; if this fire, as I believe, turns out to be the handiwork of Communists, there is nothing that shall stop us now from crushing out this murder pest with an iron fist." To a member of the Press he said, "You are seeing the beginning of a great new epoch in German history; this fire is the beginning."

Outside Germany the Communist guilt for the fire was freely doubted, as the Catholic guilt for the Great Fire of London was doubted. The German leaders displayed no such doubt. Under the direction and command of Hermann Göring the round-up of subversive citizens and disruptive organisations began at once.

When the nation went to the polls, on March 5th, of the votes cast 52 per cent. were for the Government, although the Nazi party did not command a clear majority in the House. It had nearly 44 per cent. of the total seats. This proportion was, however, not an effective factor, for the Communists were under restraint, and their 89 members could not vote against the Government. This situation caused an amount of unfriendly comment outside Germany, although in Great Britain commentators were constrained to recall how similar had been the British Parliament in the days of Sinn Fein.

At this stage in the relations of the two nations a rapprochement was eminently probable. The British did not relish Nazi methods, but they at least appreciated their necessity. The Bolshevism which Hitler and his comrades were fighting in Germany had in Russia taken an acute anti-British turn, showing itself in the singular episode of the arrest and trial of six officials of the Metropolitan-Vickers Company in Moscow. The British Government on information supplied by its ambassador took the immediate view that there was no basis for the charge on which these British nationals had been incarcerated and, as was believed, mentally tortured. A protest was sent to the Soviet Government—and resulted in an impertinent reply from M. Litvinof. This renegade Jew, who had floated to power on the blood tide of the Bolshevist revolution, treated the British Government with contempt. The only effect of his derisory reply was a display of enthusiasm in the House of Commons when the Under-Secretary for Foreign Affairs, Mr. Eden, said that in view of the treatment to which British subjects were liable in Russia, negotiations for a trade pact with that country would be broken off. The enthusiasts could not foresee that within a year the indignant young Parliamentarian would be the honoured guest in Moscow of M. Litvinof and his associates, intimating to them that he preferred the atmosphere of Moscow to that of Berlin. This change of temper towards Russia was not unfamiliar in British policy. When the Bolshevists murdered the cousin of the British King there was to be "no shaking hands with murder." Within a decade and a half even a Government predominantly Conservative was prepared to make new trade pacts with the assassins. This readiness suffered for a brief while when the British engineers were in jeopardy, but was soon restored, to enable Mr. Eden to tie Britain not only in trade, but in international relations to the Bolshevist fortunes.

Such inconsistency was naturally incomprehensible in Berlin, which had felt the menace of Bolshevism as Britain had never felt it. Whatever the truth

about the firing of the Reichstag, it was supposed by
the German Nazis to have been intended as a signal
for a Communist rising.   There was no such rising;
there was instead a period of terror by which the
Nazis made certain that what had happened in
Russia and some of the Central European States
should not happen in Germany.

The British suffer the defects of their qualities.
They are not an imaginative race.   Sheltered by
physical geography and long political tradition from
the racial clashes that are the common-places of
parts of Europe they were profoundly shocked by
what happened in Germany during that terror.   An
anti-Semitic pogrom and a political purge conducted
with the bludgeon, the whip, the knife and the gun
seemed to British minds an abrupt return to barbarism.   Such a return was far more disturbing in
Germany than were the far worse outrages that had
afflicted Russia some sixteen years before.

It was extremely difficult, and remains so, for the
British in their own islands to comprehend the
venomous hatred of the new regime in Germany for
the Jews.   In Great Britain the Jew has been more
easily assimilated into the normal governing classes
than he has been in other countries.   Except in the
East-End of London, Leeds, Manchester and a few
other manufacturing places, the Jew does not display
in England characteristics that are unmistakably
alien.   At the ports of Hull and Liverpool may be
seen occasionally families of immigrant Jews whose
manners and raiment bespeak the foreign ghettoes of

which the English have read but have not smelt or seen, but for the most part Jews move in English throngs and take their refreshment in English eating houses after the fashion of their gentile fellows. For more than one generation men whose grandfathers had pushed barrows round the square of Frankfurt have added dignity and wisdom to the House of Peers and given tone to successive governments of varied political colour. Very recently statesmen like Sir John Simon and magnates like Lord Camrose have found it necessary to deny a Jewish origin in the face of Fascist taunts, but such taunts and denials are new in our public life. Beyond the Belloc satires and Kipling's scathing and vitriolic poem "Gehazi" there was, for example, no great emotion of apprehension in Britain at the career of the late Lord Reading. The young Jew, Rufus Isaacs, after having been hammered on the Stock Exchange, attained a great legal practice, became a Minister of the Crown, was involved in a spectacular financial scandal, became Viceroy of India and later Lord Chief Justice, and left the Bench to become a director of a great commercial enterprise presided over by a fellow Jew, Lord Melchett, and, as Lord Reading, died rich in honours. The present Lord Samuel, when Palestine was given to the Jews for a national home, went there not as a Jew but as the representative of Gentile Britain, in whose name he governed Jews and Arabs alike in the mandated territory . . .

In Germany things were and are very different.

Under the Republic the Jew had come to dominate .
nearly all walks of life.   The leading disciples of the
Jew Marx were themselves Jews, but so, also, were
the leaders in finance, commerce and the arts.   After
the inversion of society caused by successive waves
of currency inflation, Jews were found to have
prospered.   Some of the estates of honoured old
German families were in Jewish possession.   The
first President of the discredited Republic, Erbert,
had been a Jew.   Wherever the strenuous ex-soldiers
who had made the Nazi regime possible might look
they found Jews in power and their own countrymen
in distress.   On the Bench, on the stage, in the
hospitals, everywhere, they found Jews employed
while non-Jewish workers and professional men
walked the streets.   It seemed to them as if an alien
parasite was eating the native race; they remembered
the Jewish murder of the Romanofs.

Germany, in short, could not comprehend the
tenderness to Jewry shown by the British Government, and dramatically displayed by the British
slaughter of Arabs in Palestine, whereas Britain could
not understand the hatred of Jewry which drove
Germans to an excess of violence and brutality.

By the middle of 1933 the new Totalitarian State
of Germany was well founded.   The Junta which
comprised Hitler, Göring, Goebbels and Hess was
secure in the supreme command.   It should have
been quite evident to anyone charged with the
conduct of foreign affairs that from this time forward
Europe was dealing with a new Germany, a

revitalised and regenerated nation not only ready but anxious to put itself in the van of the battle against Bolshevism. As early as the July the new German Government, through its War Minister, requested permission to purchase twenty-five aeroplanes in England, and was refused. This was as definite an intimation as could have been wished that the Treaty of Versailles was no longer the operative instrument it had previously been. But far from endeavouring to understand, if not to approve, the new regime in Berlin the British Foreign Office was inclined to browbeat the Hitler Government, as it had successfully browbeaten the previous Adminis- trations when Germany was in the throes of economic collapse and political debility.

At a disarmament conference on October 14th the British Foreign Secretary, Sir John Simon, made a tart speech, virtually accusing Germany of a breach of faith. Germany was demanding immediate equality in arms with France. If anybody had broken faith, it seemed to Germany that it was the Allies who had disarmed their foes under a promise of general disarmament which had not been kept. The German leaders took offence at Sir John's remarks and withdrew from the conference. Ger- many then gave notice of her resignation from the League. It was clear that if the rest of Europe would not disarm, Germany was determined to re- arm. Had British policy been wisely directed, Britain would from that moment have begun quickly to repair her own defences. If Germany was determined to rearm nothing short of a European war could stop her, and there was no disposition for such a war. If Germany armed, she would be a standing menace to Britain, whose capital and chief cities could be bombed within an hour or two by German 'planes.

It is possible that the contempt for Hitler which was expressed in the cartoons that depicted him as a kind of European clown led British statesmen to believe that his régime could not last, and that the danger from German arms was a wild imagining which could never come to actuality. It may be that the young men of Berlin were regarded as being merely so many playboys who could be, and would be, controlled by Hindenburg.

The Summer of 1934 should have dispelled any such illusion. In the month of June the personal power of Hitler was bloodily demonstrated by the famous "knight of the knife," when the unspeakable Röhm and his homosexual associates were purged by firing squads from the Nazi Party. In the August Field Marshal von Hindenburg died, and Herr Hitler became both President of the Republic and Chancellor.

When Hitler thus assumed full nominal as well as actual power, Mr. Eden had been for some two months Lord Privy Seal with special responsibilities for League Affairs. Although he had recently by his bonhomie in Moscow sealed and cemented a diplomatic and personal friendship with Germany's arch-enemy, M. Litvinof, he had a great opportunity to bring back to the common council table those German representatives who had left it in anger, for Germany let it be known that she was not unwilling to return to the League.

But Germany had not returned to the League half a year later when Herr Hitler electrified the world by announcing on March 16th, 1935, that conscription had been reintroduced into Germany and a week later told the British Foreign Secretary that Germany had now achieved parity with Great Britain in the air. This last, it is true, was no great feat, since under the pacifist MacDonald Britain's armament in the air was slight indeed. But it showed that Hitler had not only driven his foot through the fabric of the Treaty of Versailles, but had made ridiculous the deliberations of the Disarmament Conference, which had dillied and dallied over the question of whether or not Germany might be allowed samples of those arms which her neighbours were making in great quantities.

The full implications of Herr Hitler's announcement should be carefully pondered. France and Britain had both for some time been concerned at German rearmament. The Treaty was being flagrantly defied. That defiance was an adequate reason for making war on Germany, and discretion might well have dictated to the Allies that they should strike before the defiant enemy had further equipped himself.

Hitler was facing the maximum risk of his action in announcing Germany's rearmament, and that

maximum risk was war. He and the nation he
commanded must at that moment have felt ready
for war. What followed must have proved to him
that nobody else, least of all unarmed Britain, was
ready, for what followed was not punitive action but
speeches in Parliament and the hurried visit to Berlin
of the British lawyer who was Foreign Secretary.

Germany had rearmed in defiance of the Treaty
and without using the League of Nations as a medium
of conveying to the world either her intention or its
completion—and there was no retribution. Such
open contempt for Britain and France and the
League, so utterly unpunished, must have assured
the other Dictator in Rome that Mr. Eden and his
Genevan colleagues did not really mean business
when they talked of stopping the Italo-Abyssinian
War. It should also have warned Mr. Eden that the
League was a broken reed, and not a staff upon
which Britain could lean without grotesque disaster.

Wisdom after the event shows the period 1934-5
as the real nadir of British prestige. Flouted by
Russia, Italy and Germany, she turned with a high
moral gesture to Collective Security, and *there was
no Collective Security*. Her example and influence
had failed to disarm France, Poland, Czechoslovakia
and the post-Treaty States, and could not prevent
Germany from secretly and successfully rearming.

By his open breach with the Treaty Herr Hitler
had, in fact, done much to aid Europe to refashion
itself in accordance with actualities. The Treaty of
Versailles had long been recognised as an unworkable

document, largely the result of ignorant war passions. It had been framed when the mood of the victors expressed itself in the cry "Hang the Kaiser" rather than in a desire for a just and endurable peace. It contained in itself the means of its own revision, but nobody had had the courage to apply them. The German action gave the chance of a clean slate.

Unfortunately the statesmen of Britain and France could not, or would not, seize this chance, because they feared that they might be held to be condoning the methods by which the two Dictators had secured power. Britain's Minister charged with special responsibilities towards the League may well have felt honest indignation at flagrant breaches of the Treaty, but with Britain unarmed and the League only a remnant of its originally conceived self he was helpless. One would have expected him to reason, "Deplorable as these things seem to me, my country is not equipped to prevent them. Still less is she equipped to punish those responsible. How foolish, and perhaps how fatal, therefore, to indulge in scoldings and futile but provocative attempts to change the course of events."

Britain did recognise the opportunity for a new orientation of European policy to the extent of entering into a bilateral naval agreement with Germany. This agreement was reached over the heads of Italy and France, who with Britain had formed a united front at Stresa a few months before. To them it seemed a breach of good faith, a demonstration that Perfidious Albion had not changed with the years.

Actually the Naval Agreement was one of two distinct signs that Germany would welcome a closer understanding with Britain. The other was a speech delivered by Herr Hitler on May 22nd that year in which he agreed to accept the same limitation of armaments as those accepted by other Powers and announced Germany's readiness for an air agreement to supplement Locarno. He proposed, also, the gradual abolition and outlawry of weapons and methods of war contrary to the spirit of the Geneva Red Cross convention, and suggested the prohibition of air bombing outside the battle area should be extended to the outlawry of all air bombing.

Germany at that time, it was obvious, was anxious for a closer accord with the first-class Powers in Europe. What she would not tolerate was the interference of a collection of small nations at Geneva. This she held to rob her of the dignity befitting her new status. Utopists fed on the dreams of H. G. Wells may scorn and belittle any such national thought of "dignity" and "status," but Germany emerging by her own effort and courage from fifteen years of world odium which she felt to be undeserved was bound to cherish such things. Had the German psychology been then understood her very "touchiness" about status and dignity might have been turned to good account.

It would be preposterous to blame Mr. Eden for the failure of Britain to grasp and use the new mood in

Germany making for accord with Britain. He was not the head of the British Government. But he was a powerful influence at that time. The pity was that such an influence was, as we have seen, sympathetic to Russia and antipathetic to Germany.

So Hitler's offer to co-operate in an air pact to supplement the Treaty of Locarno came to nothing— and almost exactly a year after Germany's first defiance of the Treaty of Versailles came the dramatic re-entry of Germany into the Rhineland, accompanied by a denunciation of the Locarno agreement and the offer to France of a new 25 year peace pact. This was on March 7th, 1936.

By this second act Germany had again incurred punitive action by her neighbours. M. Flandin at a meeting of the League Council hastily summoned in London made it clear that the terms of the Treaty of Locarno alone would have been ample justification for any strong measures France might have taken, thought France preferred not to take any action until the Council had formally established a breach of that Treaty.

Whatever motives France might have had for her forbearance, the realists of Berlin had again successfully demonstrated that strong action by a well-armed and resolute nation would neet with no retribution, since nobody else in Europe was equipped either in arms or in national morale to take action.

As if to emphasise the significance of this demonstration Germany refused to discuss any limitation of her sovereignty in the Rhineland when Mr. Eden suggested to the German Ambassador that Herr Hitler should withdraw all but a symbolical number of troops and guarantee not to increase them nor fortify the Rhine until new pacts could be discussed. This refusal was discussed by the Locarno Powers, with Mr. Eden, now Foreign Secretary, in the Chair, and was denounced as unsatisfactory. But that was all.

There was no talk of action. There was no mention of sanctions.

The Council of the League, as if to pour the last ridicule on Geneva, distinguished itself by reaching an extraordinary conclusion. It suggested that a de-militarised zone should be set up in the German zone to be policed by international forces, of which Italy should furnish a quota. Having denounced Italy as an aggressor and a treaty-breaker over the Abyssin-ian affair, the League was now promoting her to become policeman on its behalf to watch Germany who had also broken a treaty and might become aggressive.

Never had a Foreign Secretary reported to the House of Commons so grotesque a proposal, or one so obviously destined to be refused by the nation to which it was addressed.

Between the re-entry into the Rhineland of the German troops and the conclusion of the Anglo-German naval pact the British Foreign Secretary had a unique opportunity, which could not recur, to cement the peace of the world. Hitler was offering, however sincerely need not be debated, not only a

twenty-five years' peace pact to France, but an air
Locarno to all other Powers. It was within the
competence of Mr. Eden, with the prestige which he
had established among the smaller nations at
Geneva and the position which Britain occupied in
Europe, to have pressed for—perhaps even to have
insisted upon—a complete and thorough revision
of the Treaty of Versailles. The naturally hot and
bitter temper of the immediate post-war years had
passed. Everyone was now prepared to sympathise
with the German people in their contention that the
forced Treaty was a breach of faith. Everyone
knew that the League, lacking America, Japan, and
Germany and with Italy in revolt, was not the League
of Nations at all. At that time Germany's grievances
could have been graciously redressed. Italy's quarrel
with Abyssinia could have been settled outside the
(to her) inimical atmosphere of Geneva. The abortive Disarmament Conference could have been super-
ceded by a series of agreed programmes of arms
limitation on the lines of the Anglo-German naval
agreement.

The opportunity, if realised, was not taken.
Britain, who might have taken the lead in the
pacification of Europe was left unarmed in the armed
camp to suffer a series of further humiliations. Of
these the first were the Italian victory in Abyssinia
and the episode of the questionnaire to Germany.

Italy's triumph we have already considered. The
story of the questionnaire can be more briefly told.

The British Foreign Office, with Mr. Eden in

charge, began the month of April, 1936, proudly and belligerently.   On the 7th of that month a long list of questions was despatched to the British Ambassador in Berlin for him to present formally to the German Government.   The gist of this document was:

(1) Did Germany now regard herself as being in a position to conclude genuine treaties.

(This to the Nazi Government must have seemed a wanton insult.)

*   *   *

(2) What was Germany's view of the continued maintenance in force of the still operative clauses of the Treaty of Versailles or any agreement arising out of it.

(This was tantamount to saying, "You have killed the Treaty; will you now be bound to its rotting corpse?")

*   *   *

(3) Did Germany recognise and intend to respect the existing territorial and political status of Europe except in so far as it might be subsequently modified by free negotiation and agreement?

(That is—are you going to make any wars?   If so, tell us now, so that we can be prepared to defeat you.)

*   *   *

(4) Would Germany consent to accompany the Western Air Pact with a regional agreement for the limitation of air strengths?

(Germany had already implied this readiness in her proffered acceptance of common arms limitation.)

*   *   *

(5) Would Germany be willing to conclude pacts of non-aggression with the Soviet Union, Latvia and Estonia?

(Germany had declared that friendship between her and the Bolshevists was not possible.)

*   *   *

(6) What did Germany understand by the phrase "the separation of the Covenant of the League of Nations from its basis in the Treaty of Versailles setting?"

The day after this questionnaire was despatched to Berlin it was published as a White Paper for the world's perusal.

For some days nothing happened.

On the 20th Mr. Eden was at Geneva declaring with some heat that existing sanctions must be maintained against Italy.

On the 21st Mr. J. H. Thomas told the Commons that Britain had no intention of returning any colonies to Germany and would not even discuss the return of the Mandated Territories until the demand was put forward "from other quarters."

The British Government pressed Germany for a reply. There was no reply.

Eventually in the July Mr. Eden was forced to confess that in spite of repeated pressings no reply could be extracted from Berlin. It was clear to the world that Britain's questions were being treated with quiet contempt.

This was to prove an example that was to be followed by other recipients of British queries and protests.

Until the full degradation of 1936 is appreciated, it is folly to try to weigh the wisdom or unwisdom of Britain's policy in the coming years.

Within the space of a few weeks Italy had shown open contempt for the British policy of sanctions at Geneva and Germany had shown covert contempt

II

for the British questionnaire emanating from White-hall. Germany had dared to display this contempt because she knew that the State which sent her the interrogatory was:

> A State which had displayed its ineffectiveness even to hinder, much less stop, Italy's colonial adventure.
>
> A State which, with its Allies, had twice seen Germany ignore the Treaty of Versailles without being able to take any practical steps to mark its resentment.

That Germany was ready to offer such an affront when the ineptitude of the British Foreign Office afforded the chance is easily understood, as these pages have now so often repeated, Britain in German eyes was a sleeping partner to the Franco-Soviet Pact, which had been ratified in France a few weeks before the British questionnaire was despatched.

Ignored and even derided by the major Powers, Britain was now distrusted by the smaller States. As if to symbolise to the world what happened to those who put their trust in Geneva and Mr. Eden's leadership of the League, there arrived in England as a fugitive on June 3rd the wretched Negus of Abyssinia.

It was reported in the Press that on June 5th Mr. Eden had waited upon the illustrious exile, but that the situation had not been discussed. We may be sure that it was being discussed in Tokio, Berlin and Rome. We may be equally sure that it was discussed in Madrid, where certain military officers found their patience wearing thin under the outrages of Communists, Marxists, Anarchists and the other Leftists, who, behind the camouflage of a "Pink" Government, were ruining Spain for orderly people.

In failing to realise—as he apparently did fail—that his unsuccessful Genevan policy had had as its main effect the linking of Britain to the Left-Wing States of Russia and France, Mr. Eden made it inevitable that the Spanish civil war, which after a long period of gunmen and beatings-up, effectively began on July 18th, 1936, must involve Britain in further differences with both Italy and Germany.

The beginning of the Spanish war caused the focal point of European affairs to move to the West. Twelve months later, in the July of 1937, a new war between the Japanese and the Chinese—it was not officially a war between Japan and China—brought into existence the Rome-Berlin-Tokio axis. Both of these events placed Britain in increased jeopardy, for she was still an unarmed Power, since the depleted and largely obsolete weapons she possessed were on no comparable scale with those of Germany, Italy and Japan.

The happenings of the period from the Summer of 1936 to the Spring of 1938 brought unprepared Britain time and again to the brink of war, and resulted eventually in the fall of Mr. Anthony Eden. They are happenings still fresh in all men's minds, but they must be lightly sketched here for they created the choice which lay before Britain when Mr. Chamberlain took the initiative in foreign policy, a choice still not firmly made, which it is the purpose of this book to discuss.

Chapter X

BRITAIN AND SPAIN

If the massacre of the townspeople is revolting to modern ideas, it was the normal custom (in the days of Scipio) and for many centuries thereafter, and with the Romans was a deliberate policy aimed at the moral factor rather than mere insensate slaughter. The direct blow at the civil population, who are at the seat of the hostile will, may indeed be revived by the potentialities of aircraft, which can jump, halmawise, over the armed 'men' who form the shield of the enemy nation. Such a course, if militarily practicable, is the logical one, and ruthless logic usually overcomes the humaner sentiments in a life and death struggle.

B. H. LIDDELL HART *in A Greater than Napoleon*, 1926.

THE Spanish civil war at its inception in the July of 1936 was largely presented to the consciousness of the British public as an attack on "democracy" by Spanish puppets of Italian and German dictatorship. This was a complete misconception. The Spanish Government, against which the forces of General Franco were in revolt, was one which itself dated from a revolution. It had its beginnings in the terrible time when the Monarchy was overthrown and religious establishments were put to the torch and their inhabitants to the terror. Early in 1936 various elections, with the electoral system blatantly "jerrymandered," brought into power a "Popular Front" Government under which the country was driving swiftly to greater and greater social and economic chaos. Certain army leaders, known to be anxious about the trend of events, were abruptly dismissed from their posts. General Franco, who had been made Chief of the General Staff in the previous year, was degraded and allotted the military command of the Canaries.

Under the new Government there began a regime of strikes and terrorism. Left Wing workers seized estates, churches were burnt, political clubs were sacked, lives, particularly the lives of priests and nuns, were sacrificed with the light-hearted abandon which the British public generally associates with the gangsters of filmdom.

This riot of Red outrages brought into existence the Falange Española, a fascist body which began to give the thugs of the Left—called by Señor Azaña, the Premier, "the hungered multitudes"—a taste of their own methods.

Parliamentary coups and attempts to conciliate the shop-sacking, life-taking mobs by ignoring Parliament altogether did nothing to make the situation better. That which the British were asked to look upon as "democracy" was, in reality, a regime of direct action and physical violence, red ruin and the breaking up of laws.

Britain, which had leaned against and broken a very mild British attempt at direct action in the form of a general strike, can have had no real sympathy with the direct actionists of Spain. Had the British been properly instructed and educated into the truth about Spanish factions, their temperamental sympathy would have been with the insurgents who had determined to end the terror which was masked behind the pretext of a democratic Parliamentary Government.

It was extremely significant that the Spanish Government attracted to itself the warm sympathy of Russia. There was nothing of democracy in the outlook of Moscow, with its dictatorship of the proletariat, and yet to the defence of "democracy" in Spain the Soviet forces rallied. The reason was that Spain was presented as a battleground on which the Fascists of Europe were about to fight for possession of Spain with its great command of certain strategical points.

The British Government, thanks to Mr. Eden's conduct of its foreign policy, had been newly snubbed by the two Fascist Powers. It stood in a Genevan alliance with the Governments of France and Russia, both anti-Fascist States. Had Britain stood aloof from the Spanish struggle with any implication of goodwill towards the insurgents, the harmony at Geneva would have been marred. The three accidental allies would have shown themselves divided. Britain would have been isolated.

Actually, Britain had nothing to gain and much to lose from a Bolshevist triumph in the Mediterranean sphere, and she had every reason, in her unarmed condition, to wish to retrieve the diplomatic friendship of Germany and Italy. But whatever Britain's attitude to the struggle, Italy was of necessity much concerned with Franco's fortunes. She could not with safety afford the consolidation of a Bolshevist State in Western Europe, particularly one which sat at the Western mouth of the Mediterranean Sea, nor could she permit the defeat of a

Fascist movement by a motley conglomeration of Bolshevists, Anarchists, Marxists and Communists. It was also desirable to the still infant regime in Germany that Fascism should triumph in Spain.

To British eyes the battlefields of Spain were the terrain of a civil war. To German and Italian and Russian eyes they were a theatre on which was being waged a struggle of two opposing ideas, one of which must eventually conquer Europe.

Against this, another British viewpoint must be set. If the Fascist forces triumphed in Spain, Britain would find herself facing a powerful *bloc* of nations which between them could straddle every Empire route. If Fascism as a world force included Germany, Italy, Spain and Portugal, and these nations ever acted in concert against the British world, they would have bases for their 'planes and submarines which would enable them to sever Great Britain from her Dominions and, indeed, from the whole of the outer world. Anyone who looks at a map of the world and sees where the combined possessions of those four nations are situated will grasp at once how, in an age of aeroplanes and wide-ranging submarines, they could affect a strategical command more menacing than any known to history. The Azores, the Canaries, the bases on the West Coast of Africa, the head and tail of the waterway comprising the Suez Canal, the Red Sea and the Nile —these properly used by a resolute concert of Fascist nations could present to Britain, whether with or without Allies, a situation designed to daunt the stoutest heart. It was the realisation of this which caused many persons to press for aid for the Spanish Reds.

But aid for the Spanish Reds might have meant immediate war, and for this Britain, as her statesmen had been busy telling the world, was totally unready.

In the event, Britain's policy pleased nobody. An embargo on arms and a policy of nominal "non-intervention" could have only one result. It prolonged the civil war and angered the very powers who were most to be feared.

It must be reiterated, and with great insistence, that what was at stake was Britain's own safety. There was no question, as so many sentimentalists without knowledge of the relative strengths of nations supposed, whether or not Britain from moral motives should exert financial or even physical force to ensure the victory in Spain of one contending philosophy over the other.   The only question was what Britain could do or ought to do, caught as she was in the first phase of her rearmament, to prevent herself from being embroiled in a new world war or from becoming the object of attack by some heavily armed air power while her ports and cities were still undefended and undefensible.

It would have been possible for the British Government at the start of the Spanish war to have declared that as a nation Britain had nothing whatever to do with the quarrel and would remain entirely aloof from it. This was not done, apparently because in the first weeks France took the lead by sending to Britain, on August 2nd, 1936, "a pressing appeal for the rapid adoption and rigid observance of an agreed arrangement for non-intervention in Spain." After the usual diplomatic "dickering" an exchange of formal Notes passed between London and Paris agreeing that a non-intervention arrangement was to come into force the moment the German, Italian, Portuguese and Russian Governments concurred. This exchange of Notes was accompanied by a warning from the British Government to its own subjects that if they assisted either side in Spain they not only put themselves in peril, but made it difficult for an agreed non-intervention to be reached.

It may be asked what is the difference between a declaration of aloofness from the struggle and agreement not to intercede. *It is the difference between keeping clear of a street row and helping to keep the ring.*

Far from keeping well out of the trouble zone, Mr. Eden, under pressure from Labour Leaders, sent, on August 27th, 1936, a telegram to the British Ambassador at Hendaye. In this he supported a proposal put forward by other powers that an appeal be made to both sides in Spain to mitigate as far as possible and on humanitarian grounds the horrors of war. The intention was excellent—but what mitigation of horrors could be found expedient by men fighting for their lives, and more than their lives?

Mr. Eden was at this time greatly harassed by people at home who had mastered neither the facts of recent Spanish history nor the difficulties which confronted the British Foreign Office. A conference which included the Parliamentary Labour Party, the T.U.C. and the National Executive of the Labour Party passed a resolution which not only congratulated the gunmen and gangsters of the Red forces on "cementing with their blood the foundations of liberty and democracy," but also condemned Italy, Germany and Portugal for breaking international law by supplying arms to the rebels. The foundations of liberty and democracy which had been cemented had been terrorism, chicanery and the outraging of all religious principles by those very methods and forces of disruption which had swept both Italy and Germany before Fascism and Nazism had overcome them. The resolution must have read oddly in Berlin and Rome. There is no record that Mr. Eden publicly rebuked those who took sides with the Spanish Reds in this fashion, although in the Commons on October 29th, 1936, he supported the Non-Intervention Committee in its finding that no charges of breaking any agreement had been proved against Italy, Germany or Portugal. On November 19th he went further and tartly told the Communist, Mr. Gallacher, that:

> ". . . as far as breaches (of non-intervention) are concerned, I wish to say categorically that I think there are other Governments more to blame than either Germany or Italy."

It was clear from the debate in which that speech was made that Britain tacitly recognised General

Franco's right to blockade Catalonia, but four days later it was re-affirmed that she would not grant to him the status of a belligerent. The Government's policy, said Mr. Eden, on that date (November 23rd, 1936) was "to take no part in the Spanish civil war and to give no assistance to either side." But by December 18th the Foreign Secretary told the House of Commons that "non-intervention has not realised our expectations. . . . We are searching for some means better than non-intervention; obviously the best method would be for some more effective form of control."

It will be seen how contradictory and baffling was British foreign policy—the right to blockade but no recognition as a belligerent; take no part in the war, but seek for some more effective form of control!

Had Britain bidden her own nationals not to interfere in the Spanish war, that would have been one thing; to search for something better than agreed non-intervention in the form of more effective control was quite another thing. It meant that every incident would be the cause of a British squabble with some real or fancied delinquent.

It is, indeed, difficult to understand why Britain who had decided to "take no part in the Spanish war" should seem so sedulously to look for trouble in Spanish waters. In January, 1937, the British and French Governments combined in an appeal to Berlin, Rome, Lisbon and Moscow to end foreign enlistment. The appeal was actually sent before Christmas, 1937, but not until January 5th did

Mr. Eden press the neglectful recipients in Berlin
and Rome for a reply, which was that they would
halt any aid to the combatants if other nationals
left Spain. This unsatisfactory interchange necessitated the usual saving of British face: it was declared
to be a basis for further negotiations.

In the middle of January, 1937, the indefatigible
correspondent of the *New York Time*, Ferdinand
Kuhn, Jr., unearthed a bit of secret British Cabinet
history. By about the sixth of the month it was
evident that Mr. Eden wanted a more energetic
approach to the problem of non-intervention and was
desirous of using British warships to make control
more effective. On January 8th his plan was laid
before his colleagues, who were requested to give him
new authority to assure other nations that Britain
meant business. Sir Samuel Hoare, according to the
report, objected. The matter was "left on the table,"
but within twenty-four hours opposition to the
dangerous proposal stiffened. Sir Samuel secured
the backing of the Cabinet and the bellicose plan was
abandoned.

The interchanges with Germany were proceeding
at an awkward time. Still hurt by the incident of
the unanswered questionnaire to Berlin, Mr. Eden,
through a speech to the Commons, asked Germany
to consider where she was going and suggested that
she should co-operate with the rest of Europe while
there was yet time. He declared that if Herr Hitler
persisted in his policy of economic isolation and
political antagonism there could be no question of

British political co-operation or economic aid for Germany. This drew from Herr Hitler, on the fourth anniversary of the inauguration of the Nazi regime, a frank statement of German aims. The ex-colonies must be restored, there could be no compromise with Bolshevism, the war guilt of Germany, implicit or explicit in the Treaty of Versailles, must be retracted. The British Foreign Office pondered well this ominous statement, and allowed it to be understood that no reply was planned. However, on March 2nd, when Herr Ribbentrop renewed the Colonial demand, Mr. Eden said that the Government had not considered and were not considering any transferring of the Germany territory under British control.

In the year 1938 the action of the Spanish insurgents in bombing British ships to prevent their cargoes from reaching the Red forces brought Britain several times to fever heat, but the real difficulty of the British policy, of which this was an exhibition, was apparent as early as the early months of the previous year. During the blockade of Bilbao, General Franco threatened to prevent any ship carrying food and other goods not covered by the Non-Intervention Agreement from reaching that port, which he had invested. On the situation which then arose *The Economist* made the apt comment:

> The British Government's maintenance of the principle of non-recognition of belligerency has faced them with the need to decide whether to throw overboard part of the corpus of international maritime law, or to convoy British

shipping into Bilbao in defence of British rights. They
have chosen the former, but have tried to soften the blow
by asserting that, in principle, they maintain the rights
which in practice they renounce.

The Economist also declared that Mr. Eden
"suggests that the Government on April 13th (1937)
merely kow-towed to illegal threats by a rebel, to
whom they declined to accord the status of a
belligerent."

The exact reply of the British Government to
General Franco's readiness to risk an "incident" with
Britain rather than loosen his control of the Basque
coasts was to warn shipmasters to take their cargoes
elsewhere, but even here our foreign policy was not
consistent. British warships were always handy on
the fringe of the three mile territorial water limit
when British shipmasters, despite the warning of
their Government, cared to take a risk. In May,
1937, the Basque Government persuaded the British
to afford naval protection outside those waters to
ships carrying refugees out of the Vizcayan war zone.

While this policy of blowing hot and cold was
being conducted, and in spite of the avowed intention
of taking no part in the war, the British Government
could not prevent the Left Wing sections of the
Press from calling General Franco's force "a bar-
barous invader," the writers of such comment
forgetting conveniently the barbarism of the Reds
of Guernica who had cheerfully slaughtered some
3,000 non-Reds.

By the mid-April of 1937 a system of sea patrols

had become effective. The ships of four nations were involved, with twenty-seven nations nominally co-operating in the patrolling of land and sea frontiers to prevent war supplies and volunteers from going to Spain. This led at the end of May to a very startling and awkward incident, for the German battleship *Deutschland* was bombed by Reds. As a retaliation a bombardment was made of the Spanish town of Almeira. Germany and Italy both left the Non-Intervention Committee and the naval patrol until they were assured of protection from air attacks on ships of the international coast watchers. Their action resulted on June 12th in a Four Power agreement. Unfortunately the German cruiser *Leipzig* was attacked by a submarine, and as the other Powers would not administer any retribution, Germany and Italy withdrew from this Pact, and Baron von Neurath cancelled a visit to London.

Spain was thus early worsening the relations between the Totalitarian States and their neighbours. Even in the United States, temperamentally antagonistic to the Totalitarian States, the British Foreign Secretary was strongly criticised for his vacillations. The *New York Times* of July 18th, 1937, described him as being "like a willow that bends to every breeze."

It may have been such criticism which caused a new outburst of verbal aggressiveness in Mr. Eden, for the following day he warned Italy that "this country has every intention of defending its national interests in the Mediterranean as elsewhere in the world." Italy did not seem much perturbed. In Britain those of us who had long and anxiously urged rearmament upon the tardy Government for which Mr. Eden spoke wondered with what equipment the sturdy defence of national interests was to be achieved. What was really about to happen in the Mediterranean was a diplomatic victory for Italy. The attacks by submarines on merchant ships in the Mediterranean were so frequent that a new Conference of the Powers was called, known as the Nyon Conference. In the September an accord was reached by which Britain and France were to supervise sea lanes in the entire Mediterranean, while Greece, Turkey and Russia were to patrol their own waters. Italy stood aloof. She would participate in no scheme unless and until her parity with Britain and France was recognised. In the event it *was* recognised. Italy was given a section of the Mediterranean to patrol which left no doubt in the mind of the world, and of Italians, that her insistence had overawed the other Powers. The ships of the nation which had been virtually outlawed by Geneva were the accredited policemen of a section of the East-Central Mediterranean, guarding the very points which Britain had once looked upon as her own special preserve.

This diplomatic triumph was soon to be followed by another. The belief that "democracy" was being attacked by Fascism was from the first ridiculous to anyone who knew the truth about the Reds in Spain and their conduct before the beginning of the Franco

revolt. The truth was that Bolshevism in Spain
had been counter-attacked by Fascism. This being
so, it was humanly inevitable that supporters of the
Left from France and Russia would flock to the aid
of the Spanish Reds, and that those who abhorred
the Reds and saw in their Spanish ascendancy a
danger to world order would strive equally to help
the opponents of the Reds. Any attempt to restrain
such volunteers, however laudable, was bound to
prove futile. To devout Catholics all over the
world General Franco was a defender of the Faith.
To the anti-clericals of Russia and France he was
the archetype of obscurantist tyranny. The war in
Spain could not be a private fight, for it had all the
call of a crusade, of a holy war, to thousands outside
that unhappy country. It was the very ardour of
these fanatical crusaders which threatened to make
Spain the occasion for a much wider conflict.

On October 16th, 1937, France, with the con-
currence of the British Foreign Office, put forward
a plan for the "token withdrawal" of volunteers from
each side. It was a plan not very unlike an abortive
scheme which Britain had herself tabled in the July.
The medium through which the plan was proffered
to the belligerents was the Non-Intervention Committee. It came from France and Britain and the
representatives of Italy and Germany refused to
commit themselves. Instead they displayed indignation at a statement made by the British Foreign
Secretary, Mr. Eden, in a speech delivered at
Llandudno the previous night. He had said:

12

"I, for one, should certainly not be prepared to utter criticisms of any nation which, if such conditions continue, felt compelled to resume its freedom of action."

This was taken to mean that if France chose to open the frontier and allow a flood of men and munitions into Spain for the benefit of the Reds, Mr. Eden, despite his attachment to non-intervention, would not be perturbed. The speech probably meant nothing of the kind. Indeed, Mr. Eden's words were so vague that, re-read long after their delivery, they seem to have meant singularly little at all. But in the light of his known attachment to M. Litvinof everything he said seemed to display an aversion to anything anti-Bolshevist.

At a later stage of the Conference considering the French plan, Italy's representative, Count Grandi, with German approval, offered a concession, including token withdrawals to be followed by a commission to enquire into the number of volunteers in Spain and the best means of withdrawing them. To this M. Maisky, the Bolshevist representative, had strong reservations to make. By the 26th of the month the plan was dead. France and Britain had again been publicly worsted diplomatically, and made to seem politically foolish.

In the meantime Gijon had surrendered to General Franco's forces, the siege of Oviedo had been raised, and the insurgents were masters of North-West Spain. Italy and Germany had recognised General Franco's status as a belligerent.

The Committee of Non-Intervention had proved

to the end of 1937 as futile to stay the march of events as had any of the League's various committees at the time of the Abyssinian campaign. It had, however, proved equally fruitful in causing incident after incident between the various Powers and in putting Britain into a false antithesis to Italy and Germany.

It almost seemed as if Spain were the contemptuous epilogue to Mr. Eden's earlier farce of brag and bolt. But the epilogue was more lively than the main play, for British ships were being attacked and sunk, and British nationals seized without redress.

It was not, however, in the Mediterranean that Britain's cup was to be filled with the bitter wine of Edenism. The China seas and coastlands were to be the scenes of far more galling episodes than any that fretted Britain's pride in the European waters. The contemptuous treatment which had been accorded to Britain's various Notes and Protests and plans by Italy, Germany and the Spanish insurgents was to be paralleled by Japan.

Chapter XI

THE END OF EDENISM

Palmerston conceived that the position which (Britain) had acquired justified her in meddling in all the affairs of other European countries, their internal difficulties as well as their external relations. He was popular at home for his constant upholding of British interests; but he by no means confined himself, however, to this his proper sphere, but was forward with his advice on all occasions and to all countries, whether British interests were concerned or not. In particular he was wont to lecture despotic Governments on the advantages they would derive from adopting constitutions after the British pattern. . . . While he thus acquired for his country valuable sympathies in some quarters, he roused strong suspicion in most of the Governments of Europe, and courted unnecessary rebuffs in matters over which he was not prepared to resort to arms.

DISRAELI. *By Moneypenny and Buckle, Vol. 3, Chapter VII.*

FEW political inversions more astonishing have been seen than that of the relations of Japan to Britain and Germany. Before the war of 1914-18 the German Emperor stamped the Eastern races as "the Yellow Peril." Britain took Japan as her firm ally. Within twenty years of the conclusion of that war Japan had linked herself to Germany as part of the Rome-Berlin-Tokio Axis, and was offering repeated affronts to Great Britain.

Mr. Eden, on his appointment as Foreign Secretary, inherited a difficult problem in Anglo-Japanese relations. An Anglo-Japanese Treaty was signed in 1902. It was therein agreed that in the event of either party becoming involved in war with a third Power, the other party was to remain neutral unless "any other Power or Powers should join in hostilities against that ally, when the other high contracting party will come to its assistance and will conduct the war in common and make peace in mutual agreement with it."

This Treaty recognised the special interests of Great Britain in China and of Japan in both China and Korea, with "the rights of both parties to take such measures as may be indispensable to safeguard those interests either against the aggressive action of any other Power or *in the case of disturbances in either country*."

In 1905, three years later, this Treaty was followed by the Anglo-Japanese Alliance, concluded just before the Treaty of Portsmouth which ended the Russo-Japanese War.

Japan played a notable part in the war of 1914-18 as one of the Allied Powers. In 1918 she joined Great Britain and France and the United States in sending an expedition to Siberia against the Bolshevists. The Japanese remained in Siberia longer than the other Powers. At the Washington Conference a promise was made to withdraw the Japanese troops as soon as the situation permitted. Unfortunately in March, 1920, before that withdrawal, a Bolshevist guerrilla gang massacred 700 Japanese. This same Russian Bolshevism was at that time recognised as a grave danger to British interests both in the East and the West, no less than to the interests of Japan. In 1921 Anglo-Japanese relations were greatly strengthened by the visit to Britain of Crown Prince Hirohito, the first royal prince in the direct line of descent ever to leave his native country. In the following year the visit was repaid by the Prince of Wales. There seemed every reason why the Anglo-Japanese Alliance should continue, but it was formally ended by the needs of the Washington Conference of 1921, to the open regret of both nations.*

In the June of 1931 a Japanese officer, Captain Nakamura, was murdered in Manchuria. The friction aroused between Japan and China over this incident blazed into open war three months later, when Chinese troops bombed a section of the South Manchurian Railway and attacked the Japanese guards. Japanese troops fought their way into the walled city of Mukden.

It was not until two months later that the Council of the League met in Paris to consider the dispute. There then began the complete display of the League's impotence which first caused so many of those who had given it great confidence to realise that hopes placed in it were vain. Not until six months after the fighting had begun and nine months after the murder of the Japanese officer did the League formally pass a resolution that the provisions of the Covenant were applicable to the Sino-Japanese dispute, although some four months before the passing of this resolution it had been decided to send a Commission of Inquiry, of which Lord Lytton became Chairman, to Manchuria.

There was no question of sanctions being applied against Japan, who had refused peace proposals.

*For an excellent short account of the Washington Conference and the regret caused by its ending the Anglo-Japanese Alliance, see Mrs. Dugdale's 'Life of Balfour,'' vol. 2, pages 315 *et seq*, particularly page 18.

In time the Lytton Commission reported. In the ineffectual document which issued from it full allowance was made for Japan's legitimate claims on the grounds of security and economic requirements. Her grievances were acknowledged and sympathetic consideration given to the complications which had been created by China's instability. The Commission expressed the view that events in Manchuria had so embittered relations that sooner or later conflict was inevitable. The gist of the report was, probably, a passage which read:

> It is a fact that, without declaration of war, a large area of what was indisputably Chinese territory has been forcibly seized and occupied by the armed forces of Japan, and has, in consequence, been separated from and declared independent of the rest of China. The mere restoration of the *status quo ante* would be no solution and would leave out of account the realities of the situation. The maintenance of the present regime in Manchuria would be equally unsatisfactory.

The report then outlined a suggested future for Manchuria, with foreign advisers and a gendarmerie under foreign instructors.

Japan's reply to this document was decisive. Press representatives in Tokio were informed that after a twenty-four hours' study of the Report the Japanese Foreign Office held the view that it was a fair and valuable document, but—its suggestions for a settlement were useless, as Japanese policy, clearly marked by the recognition of the new State of Manchukuo, was irrevocable and could not even be discussed with

the League. An official Japanese spokesman said
bluntly, "What is done cannot be undone: the
League does not enter into our relations with
Manchukuo."

Japan had not annexed Manchuria: she had set up
there a new independent State.

The moral indignation of Great Britain at this act
did not perturb the Japanese. They well remembered Britain's own history in China. They recalled
that in preservation of the opium trade Great Britain
in 1839 had with two frigates destroyed a fleet of
29 armed Chinese junks and conducted a lively war,
and this without the provocation that Japan had
received. That war "provided Great Britain with a
valuable territorial basis in the acquisition of Hong
Kong, and a source of increased commercial prosperity in the opening of five additional Chinese ports.
The most important fact, however, concerning the
Treaty is that it broke down the attempt of China to
maintain her diplomatic exclusiveness, and intro-
duced her, though against her will, into international
society. In China, as in India, the general effect
of British foreign policy during the years under
consideration was to extend and consolidate, both
politically and strategically, the power and prestige
of Great Britain in the Far East."*

Those who in Britain condemned Japan in 1931-32
may well have reasoned that Britain's aggression
was nearly a century earlier and that international
morals had changed and advanced. Such a plea

*"Cambridge History of British Foreign Policy," vol. 2, page 219.

would still have left Japan unmoved, for as late as April, 1885, says the work just cited:

> . . . fearing that Russia contemplated the seizure of a position on the Korean coast, Great Britain suddenly occupied Port Hamilton, without prior communication with either the suzerain State or its vassal. Though described as a temporary measure, the act was an open violation of international law and comity; and the British Foreign Office when challenged by the Chinese Government, could offer no defence except that, if Great Britain had not occupied that port, another Power would probably have done so.

In the following year Britain annexed Burma—the act of which Lord Randolph Churchill was so proud—and Japan saw China brought further under British domination.

Knowing Britain's record for forceful seizure and annexation, not only in the East but also in Africa, and remembering the clauses of the recently reluctantly abandoned Anglo-Japanese treaties, the Japanese statesmen were amazed to find their old ally refusing to recognize the new independent State of Manchukuo, which Japan had not even annexed or "acquired" as Britain had annexed Burma and "acquired" Hong Kong. Britain's refusal to acknowledge the new State turned Japan's ancient friendship into distrust and hatred.

No half-hearted action by a truncated League of Nations could stop Japan's progress in Manchuria. Arms might have stopped it. But thanks to Mr. Ramsay MacDonald and Mr. Stanley Baldwin, Britain, a Far Eastern Power, had no arms for the purpose.

It is contendable that Mr. Eden, had he seen fit, could have remedied the ill-ease between Britain and Japan when he took power at the Foreign Office. He had been closely linked in the mind of the world with M. Litvinof, the Foreign Minister of a Government which Britain had once sworn not to recognise. If he could swallow the Russian camel in this way, he might have refused to strain at the Japanese gnat. Japan's offence against morality was as nothing compared with the murderous record of Russia. Japan had, indeed, done nothing but emulate in the twentieth century Britain's example in the nineteenth, but the Russian Government had bathed Russia in blood, swamped both East and West with subversive propaganda, and outraged whatever Christian principles Great Britain still officially boasted.

Mr. Eden did not, however, choose to reverse the policy of his predecessors and recognise Manchukuo. He preferred to retain in being the high feelings between powerfully armed Japan and weak Britain.

In the July of 1937 new trouble arose between China and Japan. On December 12th, 1936 mutinous Chinese troops had kidnapped General Chiang Kai-Shek, the Premier, with the hope of forming a new Government and declaring war on Japan. The project failed, but on July 7th, 1937, while Japanese troops were conducting field exercises near Wangping, about thirty miles from Peking, Chinese troops mistook a sham attack at a bridge for a real one. Fighting occurred. The following day martial law was declared in Peking. More fighting took place, although both sides withdrew troops. On the 11th Japan ordered troops into China and on the 15th partially mobilised and moved forward reinforcements.

The previous clash which had resulted in the constitution of Manchukuo had shown that neither Britain nor any other European Power had any effective standing in the Far East, but on July 13th Mr. Eden told the Chinese and Japanese Ambassadors that he hoped neither nation would make the clash at Peking a matter of prestige. No doubt these diplomatic representatives received this hope with dignity; had they been diplomatic laymen unversed in the mysteries of foreign policy and its usages they might have been tempted to ask what business it was of Great Britain's what either side made of the incident. Britain would certainly have made some such reply if a Japanese Foreign Minister had addressed such a hope to a British and Sinn Fein representative at the time of the Irish trouble. One thing, however, was certain. Mr. Eden was not again, on Britain's behalf, going to take the lead in imposing sanctions.

It is highly important to note how strong a blow this was to the prestige of the League of Nations. Sanctions had been imposed on Italy for her action in regard to Abyssinia. They had not been imposed on Germany for her action in secretly re-arming and occupying the Rhineland. They were not to be imposed on Japan. If the League had any real basis it was a moral basis. But you cannot have a topographical morality. The German frontier was uncomfortably near to vulnerable Britain in days of high-speed bombing planes; Japan was uncomfortably far away. War with Germany provoked by sanctions would uncover the virtually defenceless forty-seven millions of people in the British Isles. War with Japan would uncover almost the whole of the Empire. Morality had to give way to expediency, and rightly so, but the basis of the League was hopelessly damaged thereby.

Between the outbreak of hostilities in the Far East in the July of 1937 and the July of 1938, when these pages are being written, Japan made rapid progress in the Chinese provinces. This volume is no place for a detailed history of that progress. It is here sufficient to say that with even her relatively weak air force and the highly mechanised army which she had created, Japan not only drove back the Chinese, but began to display force in quarters where British interests were very closely affected. Incident after incident occurred in which Britain was affronted with complete impunity, although from time to time apologies of doubtful sincerity were tendered. One of the earliest of these incidents was the bombing and machine-gunning of the British Ambassador to China by planes flying low over his easily identifiable car. This drew from London a strong protest and a request for a formal apology with assurances that such incidents would not recur. Not until a month had passed was any form of apology received, but within a very few weeks Japanese 'planes had machine-gunned cars in which members of the British embassy were travelling near to Shanghai and had killed at his post a sentry of the Royal Ulster Rifles. A victory march conducted by Japan through the Foreign Settlements was accompanied by the hauling down of the British flag.

This was the pass to which the once dominant power in the East had been reduced. The ignominy was the direct result of three things:

Britain's lack of arms.

The exposure at Geneva in 1935 of Britain's inability successfully to invoke any form of collective action against aggressive, well-armed States.

The enmity created in Japan by the British refusal to recognise the independent State of Manchukuo.

How low Britain had sunk in the world may be gauged from a speech delivered by Mr. Eden to the House of Commons on December 21st, 1937, when he said:

> Now I will come back to what is clearly our chief pre-occupation at this juncture, and that is the situation in the Far East. . .
>
> In the present conditions there are three principles which, I think, must guide us in the Far East. The first, that we must do all that we honourably can to secure the restoration of peace. The second, that we must do our full share with others in the fulfilment of our international obligations. The third, that we must protect our own interests, and, of course, British territory.
>
> There is a very important aspect of this Far Eastern

situation which is, perhaps, the only one to-day that one can view with satisfaction. It is the fact that we are constantly and daily in close consultation with the Government of the United States. Over and over again we have taken either parallel or similar action, and that in itself is an indication of the closeness of such collaboration.

I cannot say more on that subject to-night, but I would say this—it would be wrong, with the world as it is to-day, if we were to deny our own authority or belittle the firmness or significance of our friendships. This country is not without friends in the world to-day. Reference has been made to France and to the United States. It would be equally easy to make reference to that large group of countries, the Balkan Entente and the Little Entente, stretching from Turkey right through Czechoslovakia, with each member of which we have close and intimate relations of friendship.

To prove *that*—it is only necessary to draw attention to the speeches of Turkish Ministers or to the very remarkable declaration of the Rumanian Prime Minister the other day that the first item on her list of objectives was a broader development of her relations with Great Britain. . .

Most important of all are the relations of the British Commonwealth of Nations with the United States. There is not, and there cannot be, any question of treaty or of entanglements, but there is a true community of outlook, and it is that which can prove an invaluable asset in the maintenance of peace—which is the first and greatest desire of the people of the British Commonwealth and the people of the United States alike.

That passage, studied in cold blood, and away from the warm air of rhetorical delivery, is remarkable. What it really means is this:

We have lost the friendship of Japan, Germany and Italy, all well-armed nations whose enmity can be dangerous to us, but we have hopes of the friendship of Rumania and

Turkey to protect us. And, although the United States, because of its avowed policy of neutrality, cannot make treaties or enter into entanglements, we derive a mystic satisfaction from their known friendship, although we have offended their people by defaulting on our debt and are generally regarded as aching to drag them into a forbidden entanglement either in Europe or the East to save our skins at their expense.

In that speech, whether as delivered or as I have just paraphrased it, is the true yield of Great Britain from the foreign policy which can most conveniently be called Edenism. The gain to Britain is that Turkey and Rumania hope to broaden their friendship for Britain and that Britain and the United States both agree that peace is a desirable thing. Neither Turkey nor Rumania, neither France nor Russia, and no combination of any or all of them, can defend the ports of London, Liverpool, Hull and Southampton, on which we depend for our necessary food, from raiding air bombers. Many thousands of miles of ocean prevent any possible Anglo-American combination from menacing Japan, and the complete failure of President Roosevelt's "quarantine the aggressors" speech at Chicago in the Autumn of 1937 shows that no combination is possible, whether it would be effective or ineffective.

How lacking in power to set to rights the muddled and dangerous state of British international relations "Edenism" had become was amply demonstrated towards the end of 1937 by two of the strangest episodes in our diplomatic history. The first of these

was the visit of Lord Halifax to Herr Hitler. The
second was the abortive Brussels Conference. The
first was, and is here, a digression from the pre-occu-
pation with the Far East of which Mr. Eden spoke.

The visit of Lord Halifax to Germany could have
had no other purpose than that of repairing the
damage done by the Eden questionnaire and the
general line of Mr. Eden's foreign policy. It, perhaps,
signalised the first clash within the Cabinet of
Edenism and Chamberlainism. The visit was made
at the desire of Britain, not that of Germany. The
fit and proper person normally to make such a visit
to Herr Hitler would have been either the British
Ambassador to Berlin or the British Foreign Secretary in person. That another member of the
Government was selected proves beyond a per-
adventure that Mr. Eden's colleagues no longer
trusted his qualities in such circumstances as those
surrounding a talk with the head of a Totalitarian State.

It was freely said at that time that Mr. Eden was
affronted either by the project of such a visit or by
the selection of some other Minister than himself to
make it, or possibly by both. Affronted or not, he
permitted his colleague to undertake the task without
himself relinquishing Office or pressing his objections
to the point of Cabinet disruption. That the decision
to send Lord Halifax was wise cannot be doubted.
In Germany Mr. Eden would have been *persona non
grata*, and his temperament made him a doubtful
negotiator of delicate points. It had once involved
him in some friction with Signor Mussolini and led

to an altercation at the Brussels Conference with
Mr. Norman Davies of the United States.

Of the fruits of the Halifax visit the country has
never been given a clear view. Information from
private sources led knowledgeable persons to believe
that Lord Halifax was plainly told what were the
two essential German demands—the return of the
ex-colonies and a declaration from Britain that
Central Europe is a German and not a British
diplomatic concern.

The course of the visit demonstrated, to any one
who cared to deduce the obvious, that, after four
years of Edenism, Germany no longer regarded
Britain as a potentially friendly Power or as a Power
whose diplomatic feelings need be particularly considered. When Lord Halifax, a very important
British personage, an ex-Viceroy of India, arrived in
Germany there was some delay in arranging for his
despatch to Herr Hitler's country residence. When
he arrived at that country residence, the talk was
relatively brief. Both visitor and host were to go
that day to Munich. The guest was sent back by
the ordinary train, although the host was leaving a
little while afterwards in a special train that made
the journey in greater comfort and with greater
speed. It would be straining evidence to deduce
from these things that the British Minister was shown
as plainly as elementary courtesy permitted that his
standing with his German hosts was not as high as
it might have been, but it is no straining of evidence
to deduce that the German leader did not particularly

13

relish the visit and, during it, gave very little diplomatic satisfaction to his guest.

This visit took place about a fortnight after the signing at Rome of an anti-Communist Pact by Italy, Germany and Japan. Between these two events was held the Brussels Conference, which sent a deferential note to Japan asking her to submit her case to the Powers there represented. Japan quite firmly refused.

The Powers represented at Brussels derived any authority they might have from a contention that Japan had outraged the Nine Power Treaty of 1922, commonly called the Washington Treaty, and that all parties were equally bound by the Kellogg-Briand Pact of Paris of 1928. Japan declared that as her military action had been taken in defence, she had not violated these Pacts, and refused even tacitly to admit any such violation by allowing the Powers concerned to sit on her case.

As a result of this flat defiance of the Conference no further action was taken by the assembled Powers. "Collective security" had again proved futile. It had shown itself as an empty phrase at the very time that President Roosevelt had suggested to the world that the aggressor nations should be quarantined. The failure of the Conference, unfortunately, redounded to the discredit of the British Foreign Office. The Conference was unquestionably promoted by Britain, whose action was apparently influenced by the Roosevelt speech. It so happened that the present writer was in the United States when that speech was delivered and during the whole period of the convening, sitting and abandonment of the Brussels meeting. It was transparent to the most casual observer that no section of opinion in America was in favour of joining with any European power or group of Powers in an endeavour to clap handcuffs on Japan. It was also obvious that such would be the permanent attitude of the United States. A properly conducted Foreign Office in London would have known of this aspect of the situation, and, knowing it, would never have embarked upon the Brussels farce. Faulty information, it may be argued, is not the fault but the misfortune of a Foreign Secretary, but surely it is the primary duty of a Minister for Foreign Affairs to secure sound information. A secret service which is allowed merely to feed the prejudices and antagonisms of the Office or the Chief it serves is a grave danger. Under such a service a true picture of nations in swift transition, like Germany, France, Italy, Japan and Russia, can never reach the Cabinet.

It was no one clash of view which brought Mr. Eden to resignation. Even the sketchy outline of this book shows how his personality and policy had brought Britain as an international influence to nullity. The Abyssinian debacle, the folly of the German questionnaire, the repeated rebuffs suffered through the Spanish and Japanese wars, and the perpetual and increasing jeopardy in which Britain, still relatively unarmed and undefended, was compelled to stand were the measure of his unsuccess.

At awkward moments the young Foreign Minister had been superseded by others of his colleagues, by Mr. Chamberlain, by Lord Halifax. To the cheering and semi-hysterical masses who thronged the Albert Hall to pass resolutions denouncing dictatorship he seemed a crusading Galahad, but to those who knew exactly where his crusade was tending he seemed an exceedingly dangerous person. A policy which consistently drove Britain towards armed conflict with the Rome-Berlin-Tokio axis might satisfy the prejudices of those who screamed for disarmament with one breath and for action against the Dictators with the next; it could not satisfy more reasonable people who knew how vulnerable Britain was in the face of aerial and submarine attack, and who saw no reason why the millions of Britain should be sacrificed to gratify the dictatorship of Moscow and to protect a non-existent democracy in Spain.

With Mr. Eden's resignation there came an abrupt change of major foreign policy. With Lord Halifax as his Foreign Secretary, Mr. Chamberlain assumed a personal responsibility for the direction of that policy more direct than that of any other modern Premier not bearing dual office, except Mr. Lloyd George.

The basis of the new policy was expressed succinctly in a speech on July 27th when the Prime Minister declared that in his belief a democracy could be on terms of friendship with a dictatorship. It had its first practical application in the tentative agreement with Italy and withstood its first test when Germany incorporated Austria into the Reich without bloodshed in March, 1938.

Chapter XII

THE COST OF WAR AND THE PRICE OF PEACE

We must have peace, let it be a bad or a good one—though nobody dares talk of it.

DEAN SWIFT.

THE apparent causes for the development of the present position in Europe are three. The first is Britain's chivalrous, but at the same time not disinterested, folly in allowing herself to remain unarmed while Europe armed openly and Germany secretly. The second is the failure to realise that Geneva could not offer collective security if the League were not all-inclusive. The third is the failure of the victors in the Great War, working through Geneva, to redress as an act of generosity, if not of justice, the transparent grievances of Germany under the Treaty of Versailles.

To those causes all present ills can be traced. Behind those general causes was another peculiar to Great Britain. This was the strange illusion that peace was, and would remain, the universal desire. The wretched division of nations into the "haves" and the "have nots" need not of necessity presage war. It must certainly do so if the "haves" remain obdurate in the face first of appeals and next of demands for a more equitable division of territory. But even if territorial adjustments could be graciously and amicably made, there remains in the make-up of many nations, particularly those who have either suffered the odium of defeat or the chagrin of waiting long for the fulfilment of ambition, a desire for national glory achieved by triumph under arms. Italy's burning wish, cherished for more than a generation, to avenge the slaughter and mutilations of Adowa; Germany's desire to demonstrate that defeat by blockade did not imply inferiority; Japan's patent design to emulate, in the East, Britain's career of Imperial aggrandisement in the West— these are among the prime potencies that move mankind. In January, 1938, Commander Naoki Saito analysed the situation in the Far East in two blunt sentences. "An Anglo-Japanese war is a certainty. The military development of Italy, Germany and Japan would prevent Britain sending a strong fleet to the East." In Europe, Germany's march into Austria left no doubt that if war is not sought it is certainly not feared by the re-armed State.

In a world containing 55,500,000 square miles of land it is regrettable that some 2,000,000,000 people cannot live without recourse to violence, just as it is regrettable that with all the inventions and discoveries of mankind the peoples cannot live without the presence among them of social inequalities, penury, distress and uncertainty. But these things *are*. Bewail and denounce them as you will, they remain the realities of human life. Any policy which ignores them, which pretends that they are different from what they are, which underrates them, is a policy leading to disaster.

For nearly two decades after the end of the War of 1914-18 it was the fashion in England to denounce as a war monger any citizen who warned his fellows that their lack of adequate defences was itself an invitation to attack. It was also the fashion to decry as a friend of Fascism any citizen who insisted upon drawing attention to the efficiency and intensity of the warlike preparations of the Fascist States. It was as if a man said to a fellow lodger, "There are some ugly-looking fellows all round our garden armed with sawn-off shot guns and knuckle-dusters; hadn't we better get our revolvers?" and was immediately accused of being a pro-gangster.

Even more strange was the popular treatment of those who implored the nation to change with a changing outer world and concentrate above all else upon organising the imperilled community against a possible, if not a probable, day of military or economic disaster. These were denounced as foes to liberty or as the instruments of some capitalistic plot to enslave the workers. Here, indeed, was an example of that lack of imagination of which I have earlier spoken. Men surrounded by possibly hostile tribes when asked to renounce some little leisure to build a stockade and to practise manning it against assault would not so place individual liberty against communal security. Men in a garrison warned that unless short rations were contemplated the day of starvation might dawn would not so readily suspect a mysterious plot, however unevenly rations might be shared. These two analogies to the state of

Britain are not strained.   They are exceedingly close
to the reality.

This conduct in the British was at once the basis
and the result of the false policy which was pursued
before the advent of the Chamberlain Ministry.   The
community was encouraged in cherishing two beliefs.
One was that the waters still provided Britain with
a natural stockade which the navy could perpetually
man.   The other was that no attack was possible
because the Geneva nations collectively could over-
awe any potential aggressor.

Of the first of these beliefs the national mind has
now been disabused.   It has been made clear even
to slow intelligences that hundreds of aeroplanes,
each flying at or over 200 miles an hour, each carrying
many tons of bombs—high-explosive bombs, gas-
filled bombs, thermite bombs for causing fires—
despatched in "bee formation," that is, in pairs,
with one 'plane of each pair at, say, 20,000 feet and
the other at about 2,000, can not only "leap-frog"
the narrow waters and ignore a floating fleet, but
can also successfully baffle an interceptor fleet of
fighting 'planes and defy the ground defences.   Some
'planes of such an armada would be brought down,
but the percentage would be pitifully low.

The technique of the "silent approach," developed
in Barcelona, and graphically described by Mr. John
Langdon-Davies in his "Air Raid,"* which would
permit enemy 'planes to cover without noise the
last two hundred miles of their hostile flight, has

*Published by Routledge.

destroyed the last vestige of comfort from surrounding waters and guarding battleships.

The second belief, in the efficacy of Collective Security, wavered with Abyssinia and disappeared save in a very few minds with the progress of the war in China and the seizure of Austria.

In the history of the premature and abortive attempt to organise such collective security, Austria will have a specially important place. When in 1934 the then Chancellor of Austria was murdered, there was suspected an imminent danger of a Nazi coup. Signor Mussolini, without hesitation, rushed his artillery to the Brenner Pass, for to Italy at that time the preservation of the independence of Austria was vital. In March, 1938, when the Nazis took Austria, Signor Mussolini was entirely quiescent. As he said at Genoa the following week-end, much water had flowed under the bridges of the Thames, the Spree and the Tiber since 1934. The futile application of sanctions to Italy and the action of Great Britain in uttering at Stresa no warning of her intention to press on those sanctions at Geneva had linked Italy to Germany and made the independence of Austria no longer a matter of moment to her. As both these nations and their Eastern associate, Japan, were inimical to the League of Nations, and as the United States and some other nations were not of the League, Geneva could not offer collective security. It could only offer to co-ordinate its own States in opposition to the League defiers. As Germany, Italy and Japan had concentrated with great sacrifice and effort upon arming and training themselves for war, no such co-ordination could offer anything approaching security.

Collective Security, in any event, could only be a doubtful protection to the crowded forty-seven millions of Great Britain. Her situation, as this book has earlier tried to demonstrate, is unique in its danger. Before 1914 and the quick subsequent development of military aircraft, Britain could always, upon the outbreak of war, rely upon a short space of time, whether in weeks or months, in which to prepare her fighting machine. She could rely upon a few days in which to move an expeditionary force. She might count on many weeks in which to call together and prepare a citizen army, as "Kitchener's Army" was summoned and prepared. However short that time-lag, it would be sufficient to allow her allies to engage the enemy, as Belgium and France engaged the Germans in 1914.

To-day that time-lag does not exist. If Britain, as one of a group of "collective security" nations, were attacked from the air, her principal ports, the mouths through which her people are fed, would be immediately under bombardment. At best, her intaking and distributing facilities would be seriously impaired, perhaps to the point of social disorder. At worst, the nation would be suddenly plunged into the horrors hitherto known only after a long naval blockade. In addition the fourteen millions within a circle of London and the eight or more millions in the Leeds-Liverpool belt of congested townships would be subjected to heavy bombing and their water and milk supplies disrupted. The retaliatory action of the Collective Security allies would not save Britain. She would be out of the ring before the fight began. This disability for modern conflict is shared by no other European nation, for no other depends upon vast quantities of food-stuffs delivered through four key ports.

It may be said that such a "defeatist" picture would be equally true of a Britain relying upon her own defensive and retaliatory forces. We have, indeed, to face the fact that retaliatory forces cannot save, but only avenge. The hope, of course, is that if enemy pilots know that their attack will release such retaliation that they will have nowhere to which to return, they will never start, that foreign statesmen will not invite the ruin of their own people from such retaliation. In this regard the difference between national defensive and retaliatory forces and those proposed to be applied by a group of collective security allies is that the one will be loosed immediately and without hesitation while the other may fail to apply itself. To put the matter simply, if nation "A" attacks nation "B," and nation "B" has large forces, they move at once. If, however, nation "A" attacks nation "B" and nation "B" relies upon collective security, there may be a delay while responsibility for provocation or aggression is investigated, or some of the collective security nations may actually be false to their pledges and side with the attacker. We have seen such delays over the

Wal-Wal incident and the murder of the Japanese officer which launched the war in the Far East.

The whole matter can best be put bluntly, thus: against the mutual destructiveness of modern air forces there is probably no sure defence. A strong retaliatory air force and good ground defences are the first essential. The support of either diplomatically interested allies or of such nations, if any, as are prepared to take arms against aggression as such, is the desirable adjunct to national preparedness. If these fail to avert war, certain nations, until science has found a defensive counter to air bombing, will be more vulnerable than others. They must accept encounter under a very heavy natural handicap. They must offer encounter only under the most supreme necessity. Of these nations Britain is one. No individual bravery, no collective courage, can alter this circumstance, any more than individual bravery or collective courage can alter the fact that of two groups of people in a mine disaster, one may be fatally trapped and the other not. No commendable moral purpose will affect that handicap, for bombs do not distinguish between motives in combatants. God is still on the side of the heavy battalions. It is, in short, no longer defeat in war that is to be feared—it is war itself.

This being so, and only those blind to physical facts will dispute that it is so, it follows that the first duty of an Administration is to avoid provocation, to avoid any suggestion that arms will be invoked on points of punctilio, and certainly to avoid elevating any one conception of right government into a fetish. "Let us endure an hour and see injustice done," is not moral cowardice, if refusal to abide the hour may mean the eventual and permanent triumph of injustice.

If that first duty is faithfully performed, there is no reason why Britain should remain the object of suspicion and possible attack, however heavily armed Europe may continue to be, and whatever Chauvinistic ambition Japan may display, providing always that an honest attempt is made to realise and remove the true roots of antagonism in Europe which are nearly all embedded in the war and peace treaties of 1915 to 1922.

The simplest way of stating the major problem is this: Italy, Germany and Japan need and demand territorial expansion. This can only be denied to them by an ultimate reliance on the power to defeat them, not individually but collectively, in war. Hungary and Poland demand back their ravished peoples and territories. This can only be denied to them, since in principle they have the support of Germany and Germany's allies, on the same terms, reliance upon a victorious European war. Russia concurrently demands security, particularly against Japan and for her Western provinces in the Ukraine, and with Russia Germany will enter into no pact.

The expansion of Italy and Germany means that, in the spirit of the Treaty of London (1915) Italy must be given a wider field in Africa and a high status in the Mediterranean, and Germany must be given

either the old German colonies, which she contends
were taken from her by chicanery at the time of the
Armistice and the Peace, or acceptable territories in
lieu. Germany must also be permitted a full outlet
on the Black Sea. Japan must be allowed the
domination of recognised, nominally independent
States in Manchukuo and the present battle terrain
of China.

Opposition to these wide and sweeping demands
will be variously actuated. Many who would willingly
see a broad re-adjustment of territorial possessions
not only for the sake of peace but for the sake of
justice, will oppose any such adjustment if it seem
the result of blackmail or of robbery under duress
and threat of violence. Others will resist any such
demands on the grounds that their fulfilment must
place the three Totalitarian-Military States of the
Rome-Berlin-Tokio axis in a position of strategical
and economic world dominance, which will quickly
lead to an imposition upon all nations of Totalitarian
rule, and that against such a development no effective
guarantees can be extracted. Still others will maintain that Fascism in any form is an evil thing, and
far from being encouraged and strengthened by
accretions of territory and prestige, it should be re-
pressed and fought at whatever cost.

With the last contention there can be no profitable
arguing, for it really means that it would be better
for mankind to endure the agonies and destruction of
another world war, fought with new and modern
implements of terror, than to endure the thought that

people of German, Italian and Japanese stock are living under a system of Government which their majorities have chosen and support, and against which their minorities have shown no effective rebellion. It is merely an inversion of the conviction which many Fascists feel about Bolshevism. If one disagrees with the contention, one can only dispute its moral basis and suggest that the cost to civilisation of such an operation cannot have been fully and properly weighed.

To the first variety of opposition there is, perhaps, one quick and effective reply—that not until duress and threats, implicit or explicit, of violence were used did the possessive nations pay any attention whatsoever to the pleas and demands of those now demanding room for their populations to expand. If the demands are just, they are no less just for being aggressively and arrogantly made. If justice is tardily done under threat of force, the aggressive demander may be led into demanding more than justice—but it is then, surely, and not before that force should be opposed to him.

It is the remaining grounds of opposition to the suggested demands for changes of ownership and status that require the most careful scrutiny. On the rightness or otherwise of these grounds must turn Britain's choice of policy, with all that such a choice implies of national danger. Re-stated, this opposition is one of frank self-interest, which suggests that the risks or even actualities of war are to be preferred to a new series of international relationships which

will enable the Totalitarian States at their con-
venience either to conquer or dominate those who
now meet their demands.   Any concession, it is held,
made to such States will in reality be aid to their
greater arming power and a stimulation of their
predatory and subjugating ambition.   "Refuse such
demands now, and fight if necessary, for otherwise
you will have to fight when the enemy is much
better furnished with munitions and supplies." That
is the attitude, either coupled with a denial or an
acknowledgement of the justice of the demands
which are to be refused.

On this attitude several comments can be made.
If it is assumed that the demands are just, and
morally should be met—if, that is, only the expediency of the concessions is doubted—the argument
that an adjustment of territory and status only
postpones a conflict to the advantage of the potential
enemy is of doubtful validity.   It is not the potential
enemy alone who will be able to use the time gained
in preparation for armed clash.   It has also to be
demonstrated that no effective guarantees against
further avariciousness can be extracted.   It is widely
held that the word of the Totalitarian Powers to a
treaty cannot be trusted.   Not only has the Treaty
of Versailles been openly and boastfully broken by
Germany, but the integrity of Austria has been
outraged after various assurances that it would be
respected.   With these things in mind, what treaties
made after primary expansion by the "have-not"
States could be trusted? Would concessions be any

better than ineffectual "danegeld?" Low's comment
on the twenty-five year peace pact offer to France—
"What will you give me not to kick you in the
pants for, say, twenty-five years?"—comes immediately to the mind. Here is the real defeatism.
If no word can be trusted, the ultimate triumph of
superior force is inevitable. But even so, common
sense would dictate the just redress of grievances,
the extraction of guarantees and pledges, and a
readiness to take action if those guarantees and
pledges are broken.

Thus far, on the assumption that the German,
Italian and Japanese claims to expansion are
reasonable and just, all argument would seem to lie
on the side of concessions being made gracefully,
without bad blood, and certainly without protracted
reluctance.

Are the claims reasonable and just? The position
of Germany differs from that of the other two.
There can be no denial that the Treaty which rent
her possessions from her was not the Treaty that she
had been led to expect on the pre-armistice terms.
Italy, also, has a strong case, inasmuch as she was
not given all that was promised her under the Treaty
of 1915 and that a great portion of what our generation calls France is Italian by tradition and pre-
ponderance of racial stock. That portion includes
the very birthplace of the Italian liberator, Garibaldi.
What of Japan? Japan's claim to dominance in the
Far East is exactly Britain's original claim to so
much of her own Empire—that lands under the sway

14

of savagery and brigandage, whose material wealth is not exploited for the good of the human family, are legitimate lands for the acquirement of more forward people. When the forward people are themselves cooped in inadequate territories, self-preservation can know no law.

Japan, in such circumstances, may well ask who made Britain a judge of morality. Britain, having herself outgrown the need for Imperialism backed by machine guns, may retort that the world has come into a new dispensation, but until she offers signs of a change of heart by the relinquishment of her own force-gained possessions, the new dispensation will only seem to be a claim for a statute of limitations on stolen property.

With Japan, as with the European nations, a Britain superbly armed could deal arrogantly. Britain in the throes of a tardy rearmament can only urge a morality of behaviour which Japan despises and meets with a *tu quoque*.

In considering such a position there is always this to be remembered, that although the Press and the platform hurl invective at the strongly armed claimants to concessions as aggressors and blackmailers, the facts are that the Abyssinian war began with the repeated murders of, and assaults upon, Italians; the Cino-Japanese war began with the murder of Japanese; and the Spanish war began with the murder and outraging of anti-Red citizens and religionists. The ideology which brought into being and into Power the Totalitarian States was not

Fascism; it was Bolshevism, to which Fascism was the only effective answer. If Britain and the so-called democracies of the world fear Fascism, they have more to fear from its antithesis. In one aspect, Signor Mussolini or Herr Hitler may look menacingly like Attila, but from another he appears rather as a Don John of Austria saving Europe from the flood tide of an alien and devastating philosophy of government. If, in the East, Japan secures territory not only adequate for her populations' needs but also for her strategical safety, and if, in the West, Italy and Germany are able to feel secure against any combination of anti-Fascist, Russian-inspired States by the same kind of accession of territories, an epoch of world peace might well be attained, during which the progress of education, on the one hand, and the increase in mechanical destructive power, on the other hand, might end the threat of international wars for ever. Rid of the need to haggle and bicker for temporary diplomatic advantages and to exert great effort and expend great wealth on protective and mutually-threatening armaments, the leading nations of the world could then turn their combined attention to that amendment in the world's economic organisation which is the real pressing need of mankind.

The alternative—and the only alternative—is conflict, and in a new conflict no man can say where conquest will lie. No nation, however well prepared it may seem, can afford to take the risk of such hazard. Each needs peace—and peace at any price, except helotry.

Chapter XIII

MANDATES

. . . the whole of Germany's colonial Empire was taken from her and divided among the Allies. This drastic action contrasted in a marked way with the policy pursued by Bismarck when France lay at his mercy in 1871. He had encouraged her to form colonial ambitions, as an outlet for her energy and a compensation for her defeated hopes. In 1919, on the other hand, Germany—truncated, disarmed and loaded with impossible obligations—was deprived of any outlet for her energies in the non-European world.

RAMSAY MUIR, *A Brief History of Our Own Times.*

MR. CHAMBERLAIN'S policy of friendship with the totalitarian States no more means wholehearted approval of all their doings and a wish to emulate them than friendship with Russia means wholehearted approval of Bolshevism and a wish to copy it, or than friendship with the old Abyssinia meant a wholehearted approval of slavery and a wish to reintroduce it into Great Britain. It does mean a return to the sound principles of George Canning, quoted earlier as an introduction to Chapter VII of this book.

It means that, once again:

> To preserve the peace of the world is the leading object of the policy of England. For this purpose it is necessary in the first place to prevent the breaking out of new quarrels; in the second place, to compose, where it can be done by friendly mediation, existing differences; thirdly, where this is hopeless, to narrow as much as possible their range; and fourthly— *to maintain for ourselves an imperturbable neutrality in all cases where nothing occurs to affect injuriously our interests or our honour.*

Those who hold that Britain may date her decline or destruction from her failure actively to intervene by force of arms in either the Abyssinian or the Spanish wars are surely in error in desiring Britain to choose such a mid-moment for action. When Hitler in 1934 confronted the world with his first major breach of the Treaty of Versailles, the Allies might have hoped with some success to attack Germany. But for a Britain that had not re-armed to force a war on a combination of States in 1935 or later would have been disastrous. The British democracy has not been educated into the mood when it can or will fight a preventive war. Since 1918 the martial spirit has been derided and rebuked. No complete change in the national psychology would have been wrought by a call to the arms that weren't there to challenge the linked Dictators. The further Britain departed from her "imperturbable neutrality" the nearer she came to the imminent risk of defeat by aerial attack on her undefended ports and people. Now that, under Mr. Neville Chamberlain, she has returned to such neutrality, war may come, but it will not be by her provocation. The chances of disaster are lessened.

"Imperturbable neutrality" does not mean that diplomatic isolation for which certain publicists long, nor does it mean ignoring the means to world appeasement.

It is quite obvious that the two main necessities of world appeasement are:

A redistribution of the Mandates.

The conclusion of Anglo-German and Anglo-Japanese pacts on the lines of the recent Anglo-Italian agreement.

The redistribution of the Mandates is a matter on which much confusion of mind exists. The Mandated Territories were put in charge of the various Mandatory Powers by the Allied nations after the War; they are under the supervision of the League of Nations. The reason for the creation of the mandatory system was complex. After the War, despite the avowals that no territorial aggrandisement was contemplated, the victors were loth to give back the German and Turkish lands which they had conquered at great sacrifice. This reluctance was not entirely selfish. The native populations had in some cases helped the victors, and it was feared that Germany might wreak vengeance upon them. It was also feared that these lands might be used by a reviving Germany for the recruitment and training of native armies, such as Britain and France used in the last War, and as bases for planes or submarines. But perhaps the dominant emotion at the Peace conference was that Germany, a blood-guilty nation, had shown herself unfit to rule over other races. The various lands and their native populations were, therefore, placed in trusteeship with selected and appropriate victor Powers who were to administer them primarily for the good of the native inhabitants.

It was not foreseen that within twenty years these Mandates would themselves have become acute friction surfaces. Those lands that were German

are now reclaimed by Germany, who declares, with
some evidence, that they were taken from her by a
breach of faith, and who denies that she was the
blood-guilty nation. They are re-claimed by a
Germany who resents the imputation that she cannot
administer territories at least as peaceably as Britain
administers shot-shattered Palestine.

Palestine itself proffers a special problem. The
exigencies of war caused this land to be promised to
the Moslem Arabs. The necessity for wooing the
goodwill of the American Jews to the Allied cause
caused Britain to re-promise Palestine, through the
instrument of the famous Balfour Note, to the Jews.
In Lord Rothermere's witty phrase, the Promised
Land became the Twice-Promised Land.

The perpetual conflict between the Arabs and the
Jews—whom the Arabs despise as an inferior race—
would be regrettable in any circumstances. It is
both regrettable and dangerous from the viewpoint of
an Empire which contains no fewer than 100,000,000
Mohammadans. Islam does not lack for self-ap-
pointed Protectors. Germany was always avid of
the role; the Duce of Italy has assumed it. Both of
these Powers are openly antagonistic to Jewry. The
British mandate for Palestine thus perpetually
disturbs the unity of the Empire, since it affronts the
Moslem population and turns their eyes towards
other and more capable "Protectors of Islam," and
equally disturbs the good European relations between
Britain and the anti-Jewry States.

Had Britain not taken a high moral stand at

Geneva about Abyssinia and China, it would have been possible for her to deal drastically with both Palestine and the North-West frontier of her Indian Empire. She cannot do so now. In each of these regions she is handicapped in dealing with raiders, bomb-throwers and ambush layers. Her trusteeship in Palestine is proving embarrassing, expensive and dangerous, but honour and strategic need combine to prevent her relinquishing it.

Whatever be the eventual solution to the Palestinian difficulty, whether through Partition or through some other means, faith will have been broken, and the prestige of the British Empire dimmed. Until that solution is found, the British remain in a position where they can "neither govern nor get out," and where their moral authority is weakened. Indignation at the treatment meted out to Jews in Germany only draws the hot retort that instead of worrying about German Jews, Britain should worry about "the treatment of her own Jews in Palestine." It is a retort hard to counter.

With regard to the other mandated territories, those which were originally German, there can be no question of Britain's handing them to another Power. They are not hers. What she could do, however, would be to relinquish the Mandates and permit the Mandates Commission of the League to decide where they should next rest.

The objections to this course are many. The Union of South Africa cannot be expected lightly to relinquish what was once German South West Africa, and the Imperial Parliament would view apprehensively the possession by Germany of Tanganyika, which is a key point for aerial communications and of great strategical importance. Into the Mandated Territories has been directed much capital and effort by British nationals relying on the Governments not changing. To pass them or their property into German hands to be administered under an alien and mistrusted system would be tantamount to treachery. These nationals would have the same great grievance as the remnants of the expropriated Loyalists of Southern Ireland. At the same time, it is arguable whether a Mandate should ever have been regarded as a permanent mode of Government. It is not incumbent upon a trustee to maintain an obligation merely because the beneficiary demands that he shall not relinquish it, and there is certainly no implied permanence in such a relationship.

The stress of the problem can be grasped if it be imagined that Germany has demanded formally the return of the territories taken from her by defeat in war, and is threatening a new war for their ownership if an immediate satisfactory reply is not given to her request. Such an ultimatum would bring the issue to a few simple questions:

Is the retention of the Mandates an adequate cause for a destructive and possibly fatal war?

Is Britain and are the other Allied Powers who created the Mandates prepared for such a war?

Is Germany prepared to accept territory in lieu of her old possessions?

The first question must be answered individually by each student of the position. Morally it turns upon whether or not the German charges are sustained that the pre-Armistice terms were broken by the Treaty. If those charges *are* sustained, then the return of the Mandated Territories would be a bad and insufficient cause for a destructive war, unless their retention were of such overwhelming importance strategically that one piece of moral obliquity had perforce to follow another.

The second question—that of preparation—has two phases: it is not merely a question of whether Britain and her allies have sufficient arms and military resources to endure and possibly win a war with Germany and her Allies, but it is also a question whether in winning such a war the true loss would not be far greater than the apparent gain. Are the nations prepared to face such a loss?

The answer to the third question—is Germany prepared to accept territories in lieu of the old Colonies?—has yet to be explored. The argument that the demand for Colonies turns on their economic value to their possessors is valueless. We know from speeches publicly made that, in the German mind, prestige weighs as heavily as economic value. The willing ceding of territory with adequate economic value and with full acknowledgment of Germany's political status would certainly meet Germany's need. Her necessity is not only for land on which to settle some of her surplus population; it is also for an extended area in which her own currency will be valid, so that increased commerce will not depend upon increased reliance upon the command of foreign exchange. But whether meeting Germany's need in this way will also satisfy her aspiration to recover the actual lands that were rent from her, is not to be known until the question is faced practically by the statesmen concerned.

That sooner or later the demand for the ex-Colonies will be formally made we know with certainty. It is not possible for men of the type of Herr Hitler and Field-Marshal Göring to make that demand a matter of public agitation without eventually transferring plat-form and radio rhetoric to the written diplomatic word.

When that transference is made Britain's choice cannot be other than:

(a) A blunt refusal, involving the readiness to face war.

(b) A readiness to renounce the Mandates to the League for redistribution.

(c) A readiness to confer with the other Powers involved in an exploration of Germany's claims with a view to finding replacement territories which can be given and accepted without injustice.

The first course is simply an avowal that the territories demanded were taken by force of arms and will be kept, if possible, by force of arms. The second course is a plain recognition of the true responsibility of Britain and the other Mandate holders under the original terms of their trust.

In the third course lies the greatest hope of an

amicable settlement of the question. It raises, however, an issue raised by any ceding of territory to new owners or administrators.

Germany's moral claim to a return of her lost territories is based on the contention, earlier set out, that their seizure by the Allies was a breach of the pre-Armistice terms. These included, among the Fourteen Points, the agreement to:

> A free, open-minded, and absolutely impartial adjustment of all colonial claims, based upon a strict observance of the principle that in determining all such questions of sovereignty the interests of the populations concerned must have equal weight with the equitable claims of the Government whose title is to be determined.

This, as we have seen in Chapter VIII, was amplified in Wilson's "Four Point" speech, in which it was laid down that "peoples and provinces are not to be bartered about from sovereignty to sovereignty as if they were chattels or pawns in a game."

In the creation of the Mandates themselves and of such post-Treaty States as Czecho-Slovakia this principle was certainly not strictly observed. The question which civilisation in its present state has to answer is whether it is a principle which can ever be truly observed. The nations were not prepared to make war to prevent a change of ownership in Abyssinia, Austria and China. Will they be prepared to make war to honour the Wilsonian principle if it is found that war is the only alternative to the transference of territories in Africa and elsewhere to those nations which, for their survival, must have a wider sovereignty? Will the mothers of sons sacrifice them to decide by which of several alien races the affairs of certain backward tribes are to be administered?

It would seem that the hard choice before all Western nations is whether the transference of territories over the heads of their native populations must be endured for a few more generations or whether for the Wilsonian ideal all civilisation shall be again imperilled, probably with no saving of the principle at the end of the slaughter and destruction.

In a "Wilsonian" world this evil choice would not be possible, just as in a Christian world robbery and violence would not make policemen necessary. In the world as it is, land-starved nations possessing military strength are as likely to demand satisfaction of that hunger as a food-starved mob possessing staves and brickbats is likely to demand satisfaction of natural hunger. Parnell's grim assurance that you cannot set a limit to the march of a nation is, in short, as true to-day as when he uttered it.

If the demand for extra territory by those European nations whose growing populations are allied to strong arms and a readiness to challenge present ownership by force is not to be met by war, the sooner a conference of the Powers for a more equitable distribution of lands is called, the better. Britain co-operating in such a conference would be faced from the start with the knowledge that she must make certain sacrifices. Her contribution to world peace would have to be the assent to a diminution of her overseas possessions leaving her Empire no larger

than when she fought the last war. The mere
suggestion of such a diminution is sufficient to cause
a veritable howl of protest from many Britons. To
that protest the answer is the simple question whether
an attempt to readjust territories by mutual agreement, involving some sacrifice, is not better than an
attempt to prevent any readjustment by force of
arms, which would involve much greater material
sacrifices. The true patriotism would be to preserve
the economic fabric of the Empire by restoring those
accretions of territory the desire for which (immediately before we took them) we disavowed, and
not to plunge the British civilisation into deadly
hazard in order to attempt to bolster the injustices
of one war by the agonies of another.

It is declared in many quarters that the demand
for a restoration of Colonies is only another example
of "the Dictators' bluff!" We all know what the
word "bluff" means. It means the pretence to
strength that is not really possessed. The five years
devotion to re-armament which Germany has shown,
at the expense of most of the amenities of life, the
record of both Germany and Italy in the securing
of their aims despite the protests and reprimands of
the other Powers, does not look like bluff. Both
these nations are to-day nations under arms. Quite
apart from their aerial and submarine equipments,
they have instituted and maintained a national
discipline which subordinates every phase of social
life to the military readiness of the whole people.
Before mobilisation, even, Germany has under arms

three times the number of men that France has, and behind those men is a system designed to render the State into a fighting machine. As things are in 1938—on the open confession of our own Parliamentarians—the British contribution to a new group of Allies would be almost negligible. Floating navies can no longer expect unbombed harbours to receive them and the troop ships they convoy. Expeditionary forces can no longer move unbombed across narrow strips of water. Why, then, should there be any bluff by the Totalitarian States?

From the point of view of a patriotic Briton it is damnable that such a state of affairs should exist, but it does exist. It has to be faced. The statesmen who permitted Britain to remain unarmed during the vital years when potential or possible enemies were arming and the statesmen who permitted the goodwill of such nations to turn to enmity may deserve impeachment, but their mischief is done. Their initial betrayal of British security governs—or should govern—every phase of foreign policy to-day.

In the face of that mischief, Britain's choice is plain. She can deny that the Treaty of Versailles was a breach of pre-Armistice faith and invite the more heavily armed Powers of the Rome-Berlin-Tokio axis to do their worst or she can admit the original injustice and use the utmost endeavour to have it redressed without resort by the appellants to force.

Honour and discretion would, for once, seem to combine to suggest the second course.

CHAPTER XIV

WHITHER BRITAIN?

Or what king, going to make war against another king, sitteth not down first, and consulteth whether he be able with ten thousand to meet him that cometh against him with twenty thousand?

Or else, while the other is yet a great way off, he sendeth an ambassage, and desireth conditions of peace."

(*Gospel according to St. Luke*, xiv, 31-32.)

THE policy in foreign affairs of making and retaining the friendship of the major Powers, whatever their internal system of Government, which would be possible after an equitable re-distribution of territories, has the objection to it that it might lead Britain eventually into a position wherein she would stand alone in the face of a strong *bloc* prepared to break its pacts of peace with her. It is the fear of this eventuality which has caused many publicists to advocate Britain's leaping to the defence, in turn, of the Abyssinians, the Spanish Reds and the mongrel State of Czecho-Slovakia. The argument runs—lacking an all-inclusive League of Nations, Britain must turn either to the old uneasy system of a balance of Power, which will almost inevitably lead to war, or to bilateral Pacts of Peace which will prevent her being directly attacked but will not save her several coadjutors for peace from being individually attacked by strong and ruthless neighbours.

The lesson of the past twenty years has been that no all-inclusive League ready to apply force to an aggressor is possible. An attempted League has merely ended in that very uneasy balance of power which is condemned on its own lack of merits.

Any balance of power manœuvred outside Geneva must take Britain either on to the side of the avowed anti-Fascists or the avowed anti-Bolsheviks. Since Britain is neither fitted nor prepared to make war for an ideology, neither alignment is safe for her. Nor would her attachment to either side in so bitter and irreconcilable a division make for a continuance of peace. It would rather bring nearer the clash of force.

But—granted that redress is first made of national grievances—a series of bilateral pacts of mutual non-aggression is not only diplomatically possible, but politically promising. Britain and Italy on the conclusion of the war in Spain will enjoy such a Pact. The Anglo-German Naval Pact leads the way to a similar understanding between London and Berlin. Between Britain and France, Britain and Russia, Britain and Spain, Britain and Portugal such pacts are eminently possible.

Herr Hitler has more than once offered a pact of peace to France. Such offers have not been treated seriously because it is held by the French Left-Wing parties that the word of the Reich is not to be trusted and because the Franco-Soviet Pact aligns France against Fascism *as such*.

A pact between Germany and Russia is a political impossibility. It will probably remain so for many generations to come.

15

It has been widely said that an alliance between
Britain, Germany and the United States could ensure
the peace of the world far more certainly than any
League of Nations.   Such an alliance is an idle dream;
in our time it is as little possible as an all-inclusive
League.   But with Britain, France, Germany, Italy
and the other European States pledged bilaterally to
keep the peace with each other, and with the United
States maintaining its policy of neutrality, a negative
alliance would be formed of immense value.

Against broken pledges there is no defence.
Against a possible trial of strength between the
Soviet States and the Fascist States there is no protection.   These things apart, a series of diplomatically ratified friendships could give sufficient assurances of peace to enable those concerned to re-
approach the difficult business of disarmament by
agreement.   There could come into being a concourse of nations which would lack one of the main
disadvantages of the now moribund League, which
was the refusal of large sovereign States to have their
affairs adjudicated upon by a medley of small
nations each liable to be swung towards a decision in
which they had no real concern by Genevan lobby
intrigue.   Such a concourse, in addition to re-
approaching disarmament, could ease Russia of her
fear of Germany and Germany of her fear of Russia
by subsequent guarantees.

Some such solution to the European problem
Britain must press towards, and with speed.   Her
attempt, gallant as it is, to repair, in three or four

years, a fifteen year neglect of her arms and to maintain a lavish scale of social services, would be crippling at any time. During a period of contraction in world trade it imposes upon the export industries by which the nation lives a handicap which, as we have seen in the earlier chapters of this book, threatens to leave them prostrate in the race for markets.

By preparing herself against attack, Britain may prevent it, but if the period of preparation be prolonged the cost of political safety will be economic death. *A national income of £5,000,000,000 may in a time of trade depression sink to £3,000,000,000. By the natural increase of civil expenditure and the special increase of rearmament expenditure a national Budget of approximately £1,000,000,000 may as easily rise to £1,250,000,000. Add to this need the tremendous weight of Local Taxation in an era of rising rates and extensive municipal borrowing, and the ratio of total taxation to income at which the whole Governmental system becomes unworkable is reached.* Before that time, enterprise will be stifled and commercial activity stayed.

The economic incidence of re-armament does not press so heavily upon the Totalitarian States. Under their system of Government, however unpleasant it may seem to an English mind, the application of both capital and labour results in a far greater output—unit for unit—than in those democratic States which are restricted by trade union rules and the high material standard of living demanded by the general populace. It is not merely that such States can make effective a preference for guns rather than butter, it is that for the same amount of national expenditure as that allocated by a non-Totalitarian State they get more guns, just as they would get more butter. This is another way of saying that their populations put more into industry and take less out than do the populations of so-called democratic countries.

The root reason for this is, of course, that in a country like Great Britain or France or the United States the mass of workers is not prepared to labour hard for long hours for the apparent benefit of a few private capitalists and perhaps a scattered mass of unknown smaller shareholders. They have been taught to distrust any appeal to their patriotism or to their instinct of self-preservation. They have come to regard such appeals as a cunning method of exploitation.

It is true that on large private fortunes the State takes a heavy toll. It is not true that this is generally realised. It is also true that workers see capital profits being taken on the Stock Exchange by casual investors who will pay no tax thereon, and are not encouraged to labour harder for such a result.

This really means that a system such as our own, which is partly a system of private enterprise, partly a system of communal ownership and partly "Corporative," cannot afford to arm.

If, as supporters of the Left Wing seem so urgently to desire, Britain is to "try conclusions with the Dictators," Britain must enter the conflict on grossly unequal terms or she must sacrifice the very system which she is eager to protect. It is the very essence of unreason to suppose that a nation with most of its inhabitants free to help or not, as they choose, can successfully engage in either a military or an economic struggle with larger nations every one of whose citizens is devoted, willingly or unwillingly, to the national cause. It is equally unreasonable to suppose that a nation whose system of finance is based on the theory that the State must extract from the people as small a proportion of their incomes and wealth as it can manage to work upon can either arm for war or organise for trade as powerfully as a State whose finance is based on the opposite theory that the citizen himself with his wealth and his potential earning or fighting or manufacturing power is subordinate to the needs of his Government.

When, for example, talk is heard of the "bankruptcy" of the Totalitarian States there is behind the phrase an obvious confusion of thought. A private citizen who began to repudiate his debts, to live frugally, to appear shabbily clothed, might seem to be bankrupt to a normal eye, but the explanation of his conduct might be that all his resources were being turned to the enrichment of his stamp collection or his gallery of old masters. The Totalitarian States devoting their wealth to the enrichment of their arsenals may seem bankrupt to the outer world, but with mounting stores of material *and a rising level of exports*, both of which Germany has, a nation may well think of "bankruptcy" as an ambiguous word. If there is a tendency towards national bankruptcy

anywhere, one may see it in nations that have yet
to achieve a competitive level of defences for their
safety's sake and at the same time are unable to
live unless from a rapidly falling level of exports,
visible and invisible, they can procure and pay for
immense daily quantities of foodstuffs and other
necessaries.

It is, indeed, in this last position that Britain
stands. For her every consideration, selfish as well
as altruistic, urges the rapid composure of international differences leading to arrangements whereby
the piling up of competitive armaments can be stopped
without loss of security.

In facing this unpalatable fact I, for one, do not
believe in peace at any price. It may someday be
necessary that Britain should plunge all she has,
and jeopardise all that she is and has been, into
the arbitrament of war. For the salvation of her
honour or the preservation of certain vital interests,
the loss of which would mean eventual destruction,
Britain may well have to challenge any nation which
threatens or affronts her. If ever that evil day
dawns an enemy will find, as a great American wrote
years ago, that ours is "the surly English pluck, and
there is no tougher or truer, and never was and never
will be."

But surly English pluck, however true and tough,
will not deflect bombs nor miraculously provide
manna to replace the food that cannot be convoyed
or landed and distributed.

It is vital, therefore, that Britain, as it has been

the purpose of this book to urge, should shape the policy towards three main objectives:

(1) Abstention and conciliation in international affairs.
(2) Organisation for military defence, at the cost of some curtailment of individual liberty.
(3) Organisation for the recovery of overseas trade, at the sacrifice of certain traditional means of conducting and financing manufacture and commerce.

The first of these means that Britain shall take no part in any alignment for the prosecution by arms of a particular idea of Government, whether Bolshevism or Fascism; that she shall adhere to the original spirit of the Covenant of the defunct League of Nations, that a nation has a right to conduct its internal government without interference or insult from others; that she shall not attempt to resist by threat or by arms a just redress of grievances or territorial inequities.

The second objective implies much that many will find repugnant, and to which few of us in Britain would give assent were it not for the dread necessity of self defence. It implies the taking of powers by Government to ensure that supplies of necessary arms are not held up by wrangles between manufacturers and departments or by wrangles between trades unions and departments. It implies a certain measure of conscription of industry. It involves the imposition—if, indeed, it be an imposition—upon

the youth of the nation of a period of national
training and national service. That young men and
women of all classes of society should for a few years
lend themselves to be tutored in the essentials of
defence, such as a knowledge of the internal com-
bustion engine, of medical aid, of elementary field
engineering, and the like, is no hardship. If the
community were told that every able-bodied male
and female was to be given a two or three year
course of technological education at the termination
of their normal schooling, national service would
even wear the appearance to many minds of a social
boon. The second objective also involves the delegation of every citizen, of whatever age, to certain
emergency duties, or, in other words, the making
obligatory of the present voluntary duties of A.R.P.

Above all else, the organisation for military
defence must mean a re-conditioning of agriculture.
The Prime Minister was right in subject but wrong
in presentation when he said at Kettering that
Britain cannot hope to grow all the food she needs;
but Britain can grow very much more than she now
provides for her own people.

The re-conditioning of British agriculture means
far more than aids to farmers. It means that the
British consumers must be led to a diminished consumption of unnecessary foreign imports of foodstuffs. The easy method of securing this is by a
flat, straightforward tariff, prohibitive, if necessary.

Such tariffs have to them more than one objection.
They further contract the circumference of trade on

which the Chancellor takes his tax yield. It is a choice of evils. The contraction is less to be feared than the continued decline of British rural life and prosperity. It is also argued theoretically that if Britain buys less from her overseas suppliers, they will be compelled to buy fewer manufactures from Britain. The argument is fallacious. In the world's multiple bargaining there is no guarantee that our suppliers will automatically return our custom. We know well that such countries as the Argentine return directly not more than 25 per cent. of the purchasing power which we provide by our orders. We know equally well that a £ spent in the Argentine only returns about 5s. to Britain and that of the remaining 15s. much goes to countries like the United States of America which do not extensively patronise British manufactures.

Against these objections must be set the indubitable benefit of increased tariffs—even, as I have written, in some cases to the extent of prohibition—on agricultural produce. They would mean that the steady and alarming denudation of the countryside would be checked. Instead of the already bloated urban populations being further swollen, and the problem of their feeding in war time increased, they would tend to decrease. Young men and women, instead of leaving the healthy life of the country would find in it a prosperous career, no longer, thanks to the radio, the cinematograph and the ubiquitous motor-bus, a career of monotony and mental stultification. Britain's adverse balance of payments would be decreased by a possible £10,000,000 to £15,000,000 a month.

Although the country's necessities could not be wholly supplied, the gap between need and produce would be very considerably lessened, and the home-grown produce would be dispersed, whereas the imported produce depends, very largely, upon four main ports, each of which with its distributive transport, would be an immediate air target in warfare.

The re-conditioning of British agriculture would mean that the community at large would have to be content with less variation in its table stuffs. Tinned exotics might have to give place to more simple native fare. The urban standard of living would suffer. This would be unavoidable. I cannot say that the prospect of fewer pineapples and Californian peaches being consumed in Mayfair need wring the heart. The diminution of consumption in Portuguese melons, French mushrooms, Dutch tulips and the like luxuries would not seriously lessen the nation's joy of living, and nobody need grumble at having to forgo a few trivial amusements for the sake of eating English instead of Argentine beef. So with fishing. British-caught herrings could replace imported sardines without hardship. The Premier has assured us that plans are well advanced for the increase of food production if war begins. They might be put into operation immediately to the true benefit of all concerned.

Similarly, there need be no heart cries at the

prospect of large urban incomes being a little more heavily taxed to provide a prosperous countryside, on which in extremity Britain could rely for both men and means. There is no satisfaction in a situation where Road Houses flourish and farm houses decay; the patrons of the one might well suffer a little for the benefit of the other.

With the third objective, the organisation of the nation for a recovery of our necessary overseas trade I have dealt in some detail in "Can 1931 Come Again?" In that brochure I devoted far more space to the diagnosis of our malaise than to the suggestions for possible remedies. With the diagnosis there was no serious dispute among the various commentators. With the remedies there was much.

One thing is, to my mind, quite certain. It is that if Britain is to sell her goods, which pay for her necessaries, she must bring down their cost in the face of low-cost competition. To bring down costs the nation must consent, either voluntarily or under pressure, to live harder. It will not be for ever. The discipline will not mean a retrogression in standards of living. The low-cost nations will themselves pass through our own experiences of desiring and demanding a better life as the combined fruit of their labour and modern invention.

We know well why there is immediate opposition to the suggestion that the nation must live harder. The reason was apparent in a question flung out at a recent meeting of railway workers, when a spokesman asked why the system should pay one man £14,000 a year for a part-time job while hundreds were unable to secure £3 a week. It is useless to protest that if the one man forwent his £14,000 very few hundreds could be provided with the difference between their present rate and the desired £3 a week. It is useless to argue that unless a large personal reward is offered, the right calibre of man to manage an enterprise of great size cannot be tempted to sacrifice his leisure and composure in its service. The feeling remains that any sacrifice demanded of the poorer paid workers is merely a further "exploitation of labour."

A similar deterrent to accepted sacrifice for national organisation is the too apparent breakdown of the old system of economic control to handle sanely the world's wealth. The burnt coffee crops, the stored-up tin, the fish flung back into the waters, the warehouses crammed with goods which millions lack but cannot buy—these are not merely rhetorical examples from the soap-box rostrums of the Communist agitator. They are genuine symptoms of governmental and social ineptitude.

The fierce animosity of the proletariate and the salariate—as the masses are taught to call themselves —against the *rentiers* is not a vicious and blind class hatred. It is an instinctive animosity aroused by what seems injustice. It is the hatred of usury. There is no antagonism in most breasts to the payment of a just hire for the use of capital. The antagonism is to an unjust hire or to a casino-like traffic in capital that gives certain members of the community grotesque rewards for taking not

industrial but purely sporting risks. It is aversion to
the profiteer and the share-shuffler which moves the
real masses of the people to display reluctance and
resistance towards measures which affect their
standards of living, however necessary those measures
may seem for the general security and survival.

In proposing necessary immediate correctives to a
bad economic trend in "Can 1931 Come Again?" I
admitted, freely, that it may be that only a change
of system can save Britain from social catastrophe.
Equally, it may be that only a change of system
can enable Britain to arm herself against possible
aggression.

If that change of system is to come, it had better
be by the evolutionary consent of the community
than by a clash of force, such as was endured in
Russia, Italy and Germany. If that change of
system is to be avoided, it can only be by those
drastic reforms within the present system which were
projected in the earlier chapters of this book, and by
the shaping of foreign policy as Mr. Chamberlain is
shaping it and Mr. Eden to the very brink of conflict
refused to shape it.

A system of Cabinet Government which entails a
Cabinet of over a score of Departmental Chiefs
selected from rival gangs of professional politicians,
many with no proved executive ability, answerable
at every step to a motley assemblage of Parliamentarian questioners and talkers, themselves impeded
by antique forms and *punctilio*, cannot organise
a modern industrial State in competition with

rivals working under swift, central, unimpeded control.

A house divided against itself cannot stand. Britain at this time, neither living under free enterprise nor completely socialised, is chronically divided against itself. Services essential to the country's defence, such as transport, food producing, and their auxiliary activities, are left to the hazards of limited private enterprise. Their costs and conduct cannot be adapted to changing circumstances by the free play of competitive bargaining, but their earning capacity is severely limited by available custom and competition. As private profit-making enterprises they are illogically handicapped; as necessary parts of a defensive system they are permitted to languish, if not to perish. The Parliamentary system, itself unreformed though busily reforming economic relations, causes interference in half a dozen ways without ensuring a control that would at least render these services efficient for one well-defined purpose.

Such a system with its intentness upon the protection and furtherance of sectional interests, its subordination of immediate national need to party necessity and manœuvring, and its patent inability to deal preventively with emergencies before they arise cannot organise the nation—and in the present world, with competitors and possible opponents organised fully for national progress at whatever cost to the individual citizen, a nation unorganised is a nation doomed to defeat whether in trade or war.

Britain defeated in trade is a Britain starving. It

would not be so with her rivals, and therein lies one
of their greatest advantages.

To any who have done me the honour to read my
earlier writings on public affairs, this insistence upon
a more rigid national organisation will read strangely,
for the time is not long past when I was engaged in
fulminating against the evils wrought to national life
and individual happiness by unrestrained over-
organisation. There is no inconsistency. Until 1933
Britain, as I conceive, was under no direct menace.
In that year she entered a new phase. The rise of
Nazi Germany, the loss two years later of the
friendships of Italy and Japan, the inexplicable and
unforgivable failure of Ramsay MacDonald and
Earl Baldwin to re-arm their country—these took us
into an era of crises and emergency. The more
rigid organisation which I now discern as the prime
necessity of our national survival will not of necessity
make for greater happiness or greater comfort. Its
purpose will be greater security. But it may be
that an abandonment of a mode of life largely
devoted to alien amusements and a return to the
simpler values of our own tradition will neither
impair personal happiness nor diminish real comfort,
as hundreds of hikers and campers in our own and
other countries have of recent years discovered.

Whatever the effect upon the nation of an enforced
simpler life it must be faced either as the result of
self-discipline through government action or as the
result of economic collapse.

There is no question of anyone advocating the

various restrictive artificialities which constrict living
as if they were desirable. The ideal solution, to all
our troubles we all know, would be freer trade
conducted in circumstances of complete world amity.
But such an ideal is only too obviously unattainable.
To speak of it, to dream of it, to denounce anything
but that ideal as economic madness may amuse well-
meaning people, but it does not help to save the
State. Free trade is a mirage of the mind unless
there is the prospect of reciprocity of purchase, and
that prospect the policies of the Totalitarian States
and of the United States, a tariff country, render a
vain hope. It is because artificialities of trade can
only be countered and redressed by other artificialities
that methods like tariffs and bounties have to be
applied.

If, in a situation such as we are now about to
endure, the protest is raised that such artificialities
will raise the cost of living, the answer is simple.
It is that the purpose of the artificial restraints is to
diminish the consumption of the goods tariffed, not
to raise revenue from them. Let such goods be not
bought, and the cost of living will not rise. The
worst that this would mean would be not a poorer
diet, but a simpler diet, not a poorer life but a
simpler life.

The restriction of luxury and semi-luxury imports
would not be an end in itself. It would be but a
means to an end. Through the redress of an
adverse balance of payments, and the deflecting of
immediate purchasing power from the pockets of

foreign manufacturers and produce raisers to British workers and agriculturalists, the way would be opened to new trade agreements wherein those nations which find Britain a good customer would guarantee a more equitable purchase from her. It is idle to say that such agreements are themselves vicious and act in restraint of world trade; it is not with world trade but with Britain's share of world trade that we must be concerned. This selfish attitude is forced on us by our need and by the refusal of other nations to be selfless. A large share of a diminished world trade is preferable to a small share of an expanded world trade—if in the aggregate it be the larger. A diminishing share of a diminishing world trade—which is what Britain is now getting— is the worst of all. If the steady diminution is tolerated, or encouraged by a refusal to take strong measures to counteract it, the end is certain Britain impoverished will be unable to continue even her present efforts to repair her defences. The much cherished social services will go, for they will lack the means to finance them.

A thorough reform and re-organisation of both the method of Government and the means of conducting trade must be difficult in a country which has neither temperamental sympathy with compulsion nor any great trust in professional politicians. Earl Baldwin during his premiership confessed, even bewailed, that a democracy must lag two years behind a dictatorship, but neither he nor any other followed the confession by any active attempt to adjust the disadvantage. It is so much easier for politicians to offer their constituents pleasant words and benefits from the public funds than to offer them grim warnings and restrictions of power. It is also safer for the politician, until the day of ultimate reckoning arrives, when the lucky fellow may be dead or in some "cushy" job in a non-combatant service away from the wrath of the betrayed multitudes. The great prototype of Signor Mussolini and Herr Hitler, General Cromwell, found a means of dealing with an inefficient Parliament, but our time is not conducive to Cromwells.

If acute hardship or a defeat in war afflicts those fourteen or more millions within the range of greater London and the eight millions or more within the Manchester-Leeds belt, if the Clydeside suffers something approaching famine conditions, then, we may be very sure, some Cromwellian leader will make a bid for extra-Parliamentary power, whether from the Left or the Right. Then we may again see, as in 1926, armoured cars patrolling the East-End of London and, as in the immediate post-war years, Tanks in the squares of Northern cities. Acute hardship and defeat in war are not mere alarmist's bogies. A repetition of the slumps and crises of 1929-1931 would provide the first, for in those years we were neither impelled to spend heavily on arms nor had we the restored competition of Germany, who to-day, with Japan, saps our overseas markets. Defeat in war, if war came, would turn entirely upon the success or failure of the raiding bombers to destroy our ports and communications, thus prohibiting both the movement of troops and food.

Neither of these horrors may be likely, but it is the duty of reasonable men, particularly of statesmen charged with the safety of their people, to face the maximum risk. If any deny that these are the maximum risk, he deceives himself with hopes, hopes that "things will right themselves," hopes that the potential enemy is weaker than he seems, hopes that modern destructive weapons will prove less destructive than pessimists fear, hopes that economic systems different from our own will somehow break down for our benefit. Or, if not with hopes, with the superstition that Britain is somehow sacrosanct, and that what befell Carthage, Rome, Spain, Holland and Portugal cannot befall us.

Since nobody, except perhaps some half million zealots of the extreme Right or the extreme Left, wants a new Cromwell to arise as the result of hardship or defeat, other means of reform must be found, unless Britain under her present system is always to lag two years behind her rivals.

Those means are available. They rest in the hands of one man.

Chapter XV

THE POWER OF THE PREMIER

A wiser and honester Administration may draw us back to our former credit and influence abroad, from that state of contempt into which we are sunk among all our neighbours. . . . Distress from abroad, bankruptcy at home, and other circumstances of like nature and tendency, may beget universal confusion. Out of confusion order may arise; but it may be the order of a wicked tyranny, instead of the order of a just monarch. Either may happen. . . . We may be saved, indeed, by means of a very different kind.

The Idea of a Patriot King, by LORD BOLINBROKE.

ALTHOUGH it is the general boast that Britain's unwritten constitution works so admirably because it is elastic, most of us forget just how accommodating it can be.

The Prime Minister is not the elected head of the Government. He is a Minister chosen by the King to form an Administration. If he commands sufficient confidence among his colleagues to gather about him an adequate Government and to ensure the support of the Houses of Parliament for his measures, his Administration is formed. As head of the Government, his power is enormous. The size of his Cabinet is largely a matter for his own choice. The business put before the Commons is largely a matter for his decision. The use which he makes of his very wide powers is entirely a matter for his own courage and discretion.

The assiduous attention which Premiers of recent years have paid to the House of Commons would have surprised those Prime Ministers of a century ago to whom an Autumn session was a rarity.   Did he wish, a modern Premier enjoying the confidence of the country and the support of his own majority-party could, without any breach of duty, free himself and his colleagues from much of the time-wasting, action-retarding, word-spinning attendance which recent Parliaments have demanded.

Following the precedent of the last war, Mr. Neville Chamberlain could create a small inner Cabinet which could be the Nation's Council of Action, able to initiate and pursue policy as no debating committee of over twenty members can hope to do.   Subject only to the money check of the House of Commons, the Departmental Ministers could exercise far greater initiative in their own spheres, as the present Minister for War has demonstrated and the Minister for Air is demonstrating. Recurring and interminable debates on foreign policy, the constant fire of questions on matters of no moment or of such moment that no questions should be asked for world-wide report, the demand for the attendance of Departmental Ministers while affairs of narrow and sectional interest are being debated by a sparsely filled Chamber, the whipping-up of some trivial mischance into a public scandal and a Parliamentary crisis—these are the aspects of Parliamentary Government which bring the whole system to disrepute and actively hinder the vital work of government.   It would need no revolution and no legislation to remove them.   It would not even need the permission of the House itself.   All could be done by a firm exercise by the Premier of the power in him vested.

For the debate of those matters which Parliament must rightly supervise another war-time precedent could, when necessary, be followed, and secret sessions inaugurated. Such sessions, we know, are not wholly secret, but at least they prevent partial reports appearing in biased newspapers at home and abroad to the embarrassment of policy.

The scope of government by Orders in Council could be greatly widened. It is a mode much practised in the Provinces of the self-governing Dominions, where its use does not lead to any appreciable shock to the democratic spirit.

By a return to the Gladstonian technique of Parliamentary resolutions, which would eliminate the waste of time caused by the necessity for passing Bills through their many, and largely obsolete, legislative stages, much wider powers could be conferred upon the Executive without impairing the final authority of Parliament.

The "tightening up" of the legislative machine in such ways would effect an enormous improvement in the work of lessening the time-lag which Earl Baldwin rightly detected between the progress of dictatorships and that of democracies. If Mr. Chamberlain chose to do it, the news of his determination would be received by the electorate at large as gladly as was the news that the caste system of the Army was being swept away or that the dangerous office of "Minister for League Affairs" had been quietly abolished.

If the objection be raised that the creation of an inner Cabinet, the delegation to selected Departments of much of the business now piled upon an unqualified debating chamber of over six hundred members, and the various other changes of practice designed to give power and speed to the Executive constitute a sweeping change for which the electorate has given no Mandate, the answer is simple. No Mandate is needed. In any event, the "sweeping change" is by no means as sweeping as was the alteration of our relation to India when, without a Mandate of any kind, a Premier and a docile House of Commons swept away the livelihood of many thousands of Lancashire's cotton operatives.

The superstition that the mass electorate must be asked for a Mandate for every act of policy is quite recent. It has no roots in our history or tradition. The electorate, if it disapproves of the acts of an Administration, may reject the supporters of that Administration at the polls; it cannot claim to be consulted in advance whenever action must be taken.

Actually, the National Government need not fear the refusal of a Mandate for its work if it has the courage to educate the people into a realisation of what is the need. Earl Baldwin unblushingly, according to his own confession, misled the electorate because he feared that if he told the truth Labour would be returned to Office. His successor need not make the same error. The Press, the platform, the

radio are all at the disposal of Ministers in Britain,
as they are in other countries.   Hitherto, no concerted attempt has been made to use them for the
political education of the populace.

The fear has been that if the people were told that
the condition of the nation was unsatisfactory, and
a cause for acute apprehension, they would turn on
the Government for permitting such a condition to
develop.   Although Mr. Chamberlain was party to
all that happened under Mr. Ramsay MacDonald and
Earl Baldwin, and is that far implicated, he has no
special responsibility for the crisis with which he
now struggles.   He can afford to tell the truth—and
the people will accept it.   The truth surely is:

> Because of the failure to re-arm after the knowledge that
> Germany had re-armed, Britain is even yet unequipped
> for another world war.
>
> Because of the policy of "Edenism" Britain has been left
> virtually friendless in a hostile world of armed nations, with
> none but France and Russia among the first-class Powers
> as her nominal friends—France admittedly disintegrating
> under the stresses of an economic, social and financial
> breakdown; Russia in the throes of one of her periodical
> purges.
>
> Because of her inability to compete with the low-cost
> countries, Britain is rapidly losing her export trade in
> textiles, ships, coal and other major products; and
>
> Because of her need to import heavily for armaments she
> is increasing her purchases from abroad at an alarming
> rate, the adverse visible balance in 1937 being no less
> than 24 per cent. higher than in 1936, and 1938
> threatening to be much higher again, while her income
> from the invisible exports shrinks rapidly.

Because her trade is shockingly unbalanced and because the world fears that she may be involved in war, Britain's currency is losing value, which means that raw materials and imported foodstuffs will grow dearer, this again raising her costs.

Because of wilful neglect in the past, Britain's agriculture sinks further and further into decline, this accentuating the dangerous lack of balance between urban and rural populations and increasing the nation's reliance upon imported necessaries.

Because of the cumulative effect of these things, unemployment is rising, and when—as it shortly may—it over-tops the 2,000,000 figure, the unemployment fund will become again insolvent, thus throwing new burdens upon a Budget which already threatens to ask for greater sums than the national income in its shrinking condition can raise. The Fund, having to sell the gilt-edged securities which it at present holds, will help to depress the market value of British Government stocks, and so add a further weight to the forces making for falling sterling.

This conglomeration of evils, not the imaginings of mad pessimism but actualities indicated by every known set of indices, cannot be resolved or cured unless greater power of control and swift movement is given to those charged with the Government of the Nation. If that power is withheld, Britain must either stumble into a devastating war or an almost equally devastating economic collapse.

Let Mr. Chamberlain appeal to the nation to face these things, and the requisite power will not be withheld from him—for his opponents cannot argue away facts. The official Labour opposition with its infatuation for Socialism cannot, indeed, logically object to a strengthening of Central Control, although it may challenge the selection of the man or men to be entrusted with that control. The issue there would be plain—whether the country is to be entrusted to an Administration the leaders of which have shown themselves eager to plunge the British people into the horrors of a new war out of distaste for the type of Government adopted by the Totalitarian States or to an Administration which has already shown itself determined to avoid such a catastrophe until Britain's hand is forced by some immediate and vital threat to her own interests and security.

In 1916, under the stress of actual war, and again in 1931, under the pressure of economic crisis, the system of Parliamentary Government by Party wrangle was by common desire abandoned. The present emergency, with its acknowledged threat to peace and its now painfully obvious menace to British economic stability, makes the Party wrangle as dangerous and inadequate now as in the previous crisis years. It is preposterous, as Sir Oswald Mosley rightly insists, that we should pay one man £10,000 a year to govern the country and another man £2,000 a year to prevent him from doing it. The duty of the Opposition, we know, is to oppose, but the tolerance of perpetual opposition and cross-examination when every hour is of value to the work of re-arming and re-conditioning a nation in the face of menace is suicidal. If the parties and factions that make up the Parliamentary motley

cannot themselves co-operate for the attainment of
executive efficiency, it becomes the duty of the
Leader of the House to impose legitimate restraints
upon them. If he fears to do this without further
mandate, let him seek it at the election which is, by
the natural term and usages of Parliament, now
within sight.*

One thing the Munich Conference did show to the
British people was that in times of crisis action moves
from the hands of the many to the hands of one. Let
the nation realise that for a generation it must face
either a sustained crisis or a series of crises, and the
placing of executive power in the hands of the
Prime Minister of the day will not be resisted.

If some such step towards quick reform is not
taken, Mr. Chamberlain will find, and the country
will find with him, that a Parliamentary democracy,
by its very nature, *cannot arm, and in its attempt to
arm will so heavily burden the industries by which it
lives that they will cease to provide even the economic
means of survival.*

This statement, startling and grotesque as it must
seem to many minds, I will support by a short re-
statement of some of the earlier points of this book,
re-phrased and a little elaborated.

(1) The re-armament of a nation like Great Britain does
not merely mean the supply of a certain number of weapons.
It means the supply of certain weapons adequately manned
and welded into an offensive or defensive force. It is not,

*The present Parliament could retain its tenure until November, 1940,
but usage is against a Parliament remaining in office for the full term
allowed.

for example, sufficient to supply a given number of aeroplanes. They must be aeroplanes of uniform model—three or four types at most—for which uniform replacement of parts can be achieved, with uniform training for ground staff and pilots, and a uniform system of tactical and strategical manœuvre.

(2) To achieve such a supply with the necessary rapidity there must be vested in the authority which orders the weapons power to prevent manufacturers from holding up or holding back the necessary quantity, and power to reimburse those manufacturers who have either to scrap plant or provide plant for the purpose of fulfilling the demand. It was the lack of this power that caused the initial delay in aerial re-armament.

(3) The cost of such rapid re-armament will be too much for the normal annual Budget, and for the relatively small —though by comparison with normal finance actually great—borrowing powers at present given to the Government. Some portion of the cost must be born by the Budget; taxation must rise. With rising taxation the value of Government stocks to the holders falls. The cost of new borrowing will increase. With that increase the debt service, which *is* part of a normal Budget, will also increase, causing further rises in taxation. Rising taxation is an added burden on industry, making British exports less able to compete with their rivals. Profits must thus fall, and to obtain the higher yield which he needs the Chancellor must again raise his rates of taxation.

(4) The Government's ability to borrow for re-armament depends upon the willingness of lenders in a free market to lend at the offered rate of interest. If the market sees that future borrowing will be necessary, and at a higher rate— owing to the consideration set out in (3) above—money will not be forthcoming for the earlier low-interest loans. Hitherto, when a Government loan has not been met with a willing response from the market, certain Departments have

subscribed. But in times of trade recession, certain Departments are not potential subscribers for loans, but are themselves liable to be sellers of stock. The Unemployment Fund and the Post Office, for example, may be forced by the demands of their beneficiaries and depositors to realise rather than add to their investments. The failure or partial failure of a great Government loan would injure severely the credit of both the London market and sterling, a blow which neither in our present circumstances can afford to sustain.

(5) Since the supply of modern weapons must be properly manned by properly-trained personnel the Government must either offer increased rewards for service or have the power to impress men and women. As the idea of National Service has, for some reason, been repudiated by successive Governments and is felt to be distasteful to the electorate, the first must be the method. This will draw into arms, munitions and the services workers from industry and cause those that remain to demand pay on a better scale. Already in certain agricultural counties, the trained agricultural worker has begun to drift to local aerodromes, and is being replaced by imported and unskilled workers who draw the pay of the skilled type they replace. This will again add to the handicap of the exporting industries.

(6) The need to disburse money in these ways and to raise it partly by taxation and partly by loans at rising rates of interest must, as has been stated, increase taxation. Increased taxation will cripple and may largely eliminate the *rentier* and *semi-rentier* classes of society. If it be assumed that their purchasing power is merely transferred to other classes of resident Britons, the effect will be too unbalance employment and throw great strain upon certain municipalities. If, for instance, money is taken from the *rentiers* of London and the South to go to munition workers in the North, the Southern Councils will find the yield from rates falling. They will have to increase assessments or

rates, or both. This will bear hardly upon their own industries and tradespeople. But much of the purchasing power
taken from the *rentiers* may not go to British workers. It
may go to American aircraft builders or foreign suppliers of
necessary raw material, who may not increase their own
purchases from Britain. This will tend still further to
unbalance the trading position of the country, and to drive
sterling further down, with the usual "snow-ball" effects
upon imported raw materials and necessary foodstuffs.

If these points are sound, it may be asked, how
comes it that what relatively prosperous Britain is
said to be unable to do, the impoverished Totalitarian
States are doing? The answer is that with re-armament as with their export industries, the Totalitarian
States can produce far more cheaply than we. They
can produce far more cheaply because their workers
work longer and harder for a lower standard of living,
and because their peoples are controlled and directed
to one end—the equipment of the State.

A trader who gives himself little leisure, works
hard and lives sparingly will—other things being
equal—always drive from business a rival who
insists on generous leisure, works half-heartedly and
lives expensively. So it is with nations.

The ultimate questions which Britain has to face
are these. Can a Prime Minister, under our present
system, exercise sufficient power to organise the
country in such a way that it can compete with its
highly organised, hard living, ambitious rivals, both
in defences and trade? If he cannot, dare Britain
persist in a system which so handicaps her?

It is not a question of "butter or guns?" It is not

a question of "liberty or discipline?" It is a question
of whether the forty-seven millions in these Islands
will submit to the sacrifice of a little leisure, individual
liberty and comfort to try to maintain their freedom
as a State and their prosperity as a nation, or
whether they will insist upon maintaining a decayed
Parliamentary system, declared to be inefficient by
its own supporters, and an uneconomic mode of
living, knowing from the events of their recent
history and the unmistakable signs about them that
these are leading them to irremediable material
hardship and may plunge them into military disaster
and defeat.

INDEX